MW01267711

The
Paisley Palate
Cookbook

Inspirations for the Eclectic Table

Jennifer Syler

Jennifer Syler
The Paisley Palate Cookbook

ISBN-13: 978-1490395852
ISBN-10: 1490395857

Photography, Design and Layout
by Jennifer Syler

Formatting, Typesetting and Editing
by Bradley Syler

To my husband Brad

&

In loving memory of my friend Jeet Pradhan

Table of Contents

Note: All recipes are meat free. Many are also vegan, gluten free or easily adapted to such preferences. All recipes that are vegan or gluten free are noted.

INTRODUCTION

Like so many others, muddled origins and present day accessibility to distant cultures have shaped me into somewhat of a culinary vagabond. My parents, both remarkable cooks, raised me on a fusion of influences from their own cultural combines of Japanese, Portuguese, Scottish, English and assorted others. Growing up, we lived all over the U.S. and good food was a main stay in my childhood home. Meals ran the gamut from stir-fry to cabbage rolls to chili to roasts to latkes to cioppino…but rice…always rice! Later in life, my husband's career led me to the Middle East and then to India where, through friendships formed over the stovetop, cuisines I had once considered unapproachable eventually became my norm. This book began as simply a place to collect my tried and true favorite recipes, the ones I looked forward to making and left me feeling most content after eating. Of course in the end, it is the stories surrounding the recipes that truly make them my favorites. Food, real food anyway, has the ability to reveal our commonalities and connect people in a way few things can. Our connection to food is intricate and beautiful in that the foods we prepare and the reasons we prepare them the way we do tell our story. Each of our stories is unique but inevitably interwoven with the stories of others. As we become aware of these points of interconnection, our likenesses outshine our trivial differences and we evolve from simply feeding ourselves to truly connecting with and nourishing one another.

Over the course of the last century, many of us have fallen away from the nourishing tradition of preparing our own food. We've devalued this tradition in favor of fast-paced modern living, a shift in values that has cost us our physical health, peace of mind and access to our capacity to nurture ourselves as well as one another. Many people these days feel a complete disconnect from their ability to satisfy their primary need to eat well even viewing the act as a difficult or mundane chore. The connection to our capacity to nurture is essential to truly appreciate what it is we consume and affirm our connection to source. The food we eat and the mindset with which it is prepared nourishes all levels of our being. When we lovingly devote time and energy to preparing and eating our food, we are nourished physically, mentally, emotionally and spiritually. Our mind and senses grow sharper, and memories are recalled which trigger emotions that connect us to the food's history. The act aligns us with our own natural rhythms and strengthens our sense of wellbeing. The spirit is lightened and infused with joy. The food and all those that consume it share in this joy thus a vibrant cycle of affection and appreciation is nurtured. It is a tradition worth returning to.

The recipes in this book aren't fussy or ostentatious. They aren't meant to impress with fancy techniques or hard to find ingredients, just the opposite, they are true everyday foods made from simple, wholesome ingredients. Most recipes should be viewed as rough guidelines with plenty of space for alteration to suit personal preferences. Some recipes, especially the ones with an Indian influence, may appear complicated due to the sheer number of ingredients, but the ingredients should be easily found at your local grocer these days, and the cooking processes are generally quick and flexible.

It's my hope that this book will inspire you to reclaim the kitchen as a sacred space and rediscover the preparation of food as a practice to awaken awareness, vitality and gratitude for the world around you. I also hope that it will help you recall old and create new stories of your own so that you may feel connected and nourished from the inside out.

COMMONLY USED INGREDIENTS

ASAFOETIDA

A spice produced from the dried sap extract of the Ferula asafoetida root, a perennial herb native to the Middle East and member of the parsley, dill, caraway, fennel and celery family. The light amber colored spice is commonly found in tiny resin briquette or powdered form. It possesses a potent sulfur aroma that earned it the nicknames "Devil's Dung" and "Stink Finger." Used as both a digestive aid and flavor enhancer, it possesses a sharp, bitter flavor that, when cooked, mimics that of garlic and onion thus making it a common ingredient in ayurvedic cooking where such ingredients are limited or excluded. It is considered a crucial ingredient in many Indian curries as well as in all kinds of pickles, relishes, chutneys and papads.

ATTA

A term that implies a finely ground whole grain flour. Traditionally made from whole berries of hard or semi-hard wheat varieties, this whole grain flour is often used to make south Asian flat breads such as chapatti and paratha. These days,

atta made from many grain varieties can be found.

BASMATI RICE

A long-grained rice that is grain aged to develop superior taste, perfume like fragrance and a fine texture that cooks up lighter and fluffier than most rice varieties. It is predominantly grown along the foothills of the Himalayas and is available in white and brown varieties.

BESAN FLOUR

A cereal flour made from either raw or roasted garbanzo beans. Also known as gram, chickpea, garbanzo or channa dal flour, besan is high in protein and gluten free. This pale yellow colored flour is a staple of Indian, Pakistani, Bangladeshi, and Moroccan cuisine.

BLACK SALT

An Indian mineral salt with a pinkish-grey color. It has a

distinct egg-like flavor and pungent sulfurous aroma. Though not interchangeable with sea salt or table salt, small amounts may be used in place of or in conjunction with such salts to add an additional layer of flavor to chutneys, raitas, pickles, fresh cut fruit and savory snacks. It is a predominant flavor in chaat masala, the Indian snack spice blend.

BROWN LENTILS

Small, flat and greenish-brown, these lentils have a mild flavor and mealy texture. They retain their shape relatively well during cooking and are suitable for dishes such as soups, vegetable bakes and casseroles.

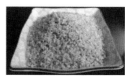

BULGAR WHEAT

Kernels of whole wheat that are soaked, parboiled, dried and then cracked. This grain has a sweet nutty flavor, slightly chewy texture and requires little to no cooking time. Used in many Middle Eastern and Mediterranean dishes, it can also be used in most dishes calling for rice or couscous.

CARDAMOM

A spice commonly used in Middle Eastern, African and some Scandinavian cuisines. This member of the ginger family is frequently called the "Queen of Spices" due to its strong but pleasant taste and aroma as well as its long list of health benefits. Varieties of green or black pods encase the tiny black seeds whose exotic, spicy-sweet flavor lends itself to both sweet and savory dishes.

CHICKPEAS

The most versatile and widely consumed legume in the world. The two most predominant varieties are garbanzo (often referred to as garbanzo beans) and desi. The garbanzo variety has a semi-smooth, creamy white coat while the desi variety is a smaller seed with a wrinkly, dark brown coat. Both varieties have a firm texture and a flavor resembling something between a chestnut and a walnut.

CHILI

The fruit of the flowering capsicum plants originally cultivated in the Americas. The pods are used in fresh, dried or pickled state to add flavor and heat to a dish. Even small amounts provide tongue tingling warmth. Their many health benefits include increased circulation and boosted immune function.

CORIANDER

An annual herb in the Apiaceae family that also goes by the names cilantro, Chinese parsley or dhania. Native to the Mediterranean region, it is now cultivated and used as a common ingredient in many parts of Asia, Latin America, Africa, India and Scandinavia. The leaves, stems, roots and berries (which are dried and called seeds) of this herb are all used in cooking. Coriander provides a sweet fragrance and distinct, fresh citrus flavor that make the herb a favorite garnish and flavor enhancer.

CUMIN

A spice originally from the Mediterranean region and later used extensively by the Greeks, Romans, Persians and Egyptians for both culinary and medicinal purposes. It is a member of the same family as caraway, parsley and dill and has a cooling effect on the body. With a peppery, slightly citrusy flavor, it is a common inclusion in chili powders and curry powders.

CURRY LEAVES

Sometimes called sweet neem leaves, these faintly aromatic leaves of the curry tree are used extensively in Southeast Asian cuisine. The whole or torn leaves are used as a tempering agent for curries, dals, rasams, sambar and chutneys while the dry roasted leaves are often found in spice powders. They possess numerous homeopathic qualities and are therefore highly valued in Ayurvedic medicine.

CURRY POWDER

Any of numerous spice blends based on South Asian Cuisine. Spices commonly included in today's commercial blends are cumin, coriander, ginger, turmeric, fenugreek and chili.

DRIED MANGO POWDER

A spice made of finely ground unripe mango pieces that have been sun dried. It has a slightly sweet, very tart flavor akin to tamarind and is used as a souring agent in many Indian curries, chutneys and soups.

DRUMSTICK

Immature seed pods of the Moringa oleifera tree, the most common tree in India. The long, slender and triangular shaped pods have a taste similar to that of green beans and okra and are included in many soups and stews of Asian cuisines.

FENUGREEK

An annual plant grown for centuries in India, the Mediterranean and North Africa. The small round leaves can be used fresh or dried as an herb. The stems and leaves can be harvested as micro greens, referred to as methi, and used as a salad green. The cube shaped, golden colored seeds of the plant have a slightly bitter taste and should be sprouted or lightly roasted prior to use in a dish. Once roasted, the seeds can be used whole or in powdered form to impart a mellow, tangy flavor in curries, soups, vegetables and spice mixes.

FETA

A crumbly, soft white cheese traditionally made of sheep's milk or a combination of sheep and goat's milk. It is pickled in a brine to render a salty, tangy, sharp flavor suitable for most salads, pastries and sandwiches.

The Paisley Palate Cookbook

GARAM MASALA

A pungent spice blend common in North Indian and South Asian cuisines. Though its composition varies from region to region and cook to cook, common ingredients include coriander seeds, cumin seeds, black peppercorn, ginger, cardamom, cloves, cinnamon and bay leaves. The individual spices are usually pre-roasted to bring out their flavors, which means the mixture can be added at the very end of the dish's preparation.

GHEE

Clarified butter, or pure butterfat, which is made by heating butter until it's components separate out by density. As the water evaporates, some of the milk solids sink to the bottom, brown and infuse their flavor into the butterfat. The rest of the milk solids float to the top and form a foam layer that is then skimmed off. The pure butterfat is then poured off and allowed to set into a solid as it cools. Ghee is shelf stable and possesses a much higher smoke point than whole butter. It is highly regarded in Indian culture and ayurvedic medicine as the essence of milk, and has numerous culinary, therapeutic and religious applications.

HAKKA NOODLES

Any of a variety of noodles taking strong influence from the Hakka community in the Fujian Province in China. Traditionally thin, flat rice noodles, today's Indo-Chinese Hakka Noodles are more commonly made from Durum flour with or without eggs.

JAGGERY

A natural sweetening agent commonly used in parts of Asia, Africa, Latin America and the Caribbean. Made from either raw sugar cane juice or palm sap, the liquid is boiled in iron pans then cooled in block molds. The absence of any additional processing means it retains its molasses flavor as well as much of its natural vitamin and mineral content.

KALAMATA OLIVES

Almond-shaped, plump, dark purple olives named after the southern Greek city of Kalamata. Typically preserved in a brine or wine vinegar-brine mixture, they have a salty, tart flavor with a mildly bitter aftertaste. They make a nice table olive and are a common inclusion of many Mediterranean salads, sauces and spreads.

KIDNEY BEANS

Dark red beans with a signature kidney shape. Originating in Peru, today's kidney beans are popular in cultures the world over. Their ability to hold their shape during cooking and absorb surrounding flavors well make them a favorite for simmered dishes such as American chili and North Indian curries. Cannellini beans are white colored kidney beans. The varieties can be directly substituted for one another.

MASOOR DAL

Masoor lentils that have been skinned and split. Though very flavorful, these small salmon colored lentils have a propensity to disintegrate into a thick, dry, light yellow purée when cooked making them most appropriate for use in thick soups and Indian dal dishes.

MUNG BEANS

Tiny, bright green, oval shaped beans that are popular in Southeast Asia. The whole beans cook quickly and require no pre-soaking. They can be quick-sprouted and eaten in salads or cooked in soups or stews. Longer sprouted beans are often added to Asian steamed buns and stir-fries. They are highly regarded in Ayurvedic medicine for their nutritional potency and easy digestibility.

MUNG DAL

Mung beans that have been stripped of their bright green outer hull and split. The light yellow dal cooks quickly and is the gentlest pulse in regards to demand on the digestive system thus making it a popular choice in dishes like simple kitchadi. It can be cooked down, pounded into a dry paste and used as the basis for jellies, crepe batters and noodles. The paste can also be sweetened and used in dessert items, much like red bean paste.

MUSTARD SEEDS

Seeds from the cruciferous mustard plant, related to broccoli, Brussels sprouts and cabbage. They are available in yellow, brown or black varieties and can be used whole or powdered. The black and brown seeds possess a more pungent, acrid taste and can be used interchangeably. The milder, yellow variety is commonly used to make American yellow mustard.

PANEER

An unripened Indian cheese, sometimes called curd cheese or cottage cheese, made by pressing together the solids of curdled cow's milk. It has an extremely mild flavor, low fat content, high water content and a non-melty, firm tofu-like texture that makes it a very versatile ingredient common to Indian cuisine.

PEARL BARLEY

Barley grain with its outer most hull removed. The production of pearl barley entails various degrees of polishing or "pearling" and may also include the removal of the grain's bran layer or even parts of its endosperm layer. The pearly white kernels have a longer shelf life and shorter cooking time than hulled barley though the processing does render them less than a whole grain thus less nutritious.

SEMOLINA

The coarsely ground endosperm of wheat. It ranges in color from off-white to yellow depending on the variety of wheat used and is most commonly used in the preparation of hot cereals, Middle Eastern cakes, and artesian breads and desserts.

TAHINI

A paste made from ground, hulled sesame seeds. It has a strong nutty flavor, oily consistency and is popular in eastern Mediterranean cuisine.

TOOR DAL

Green pigeon peas stripped of their outer hull and split. Also called arhar dal or toor dal, it is one of the most popular pulses in the Indian diet and an important source of protein in a mostly vegetarian diet.

TURMERIC

A spice made from grinding the roots of the Curcuma longa plant. Sometimes called the "poor man's saffron" or the "golden spice of life," it is the primary ingredient in curry powder and frequently included in much of Asia's cuisine. It has a vibrant yellow color and a warm, pungent flavor, both of which are attributes of curcumin, a compound shown to have antioxidant, anti-inflammatory, antibacterial, stomach-soothing, and liver and heart-protecting affects.

SAMBAR POWDER

A pungent and aromatic dry spice mixture whose basic ingredients include red chili, coriander seed, fenugreek seed, black peppercorns, cumin seed, mustard seed, turmeric and sometimes dal. The mixture is most commonly used to flavor sambar, a south Indian vegetable stew, but can also be used to add unique flavor to any dish that calls for chili powder.

STAR ANISE

The star shaped seedpods of a small evergreen tree native to southwest China, now also grown in Japan and Southeast Asia. Anethole oil gives star anise the warm, sweet, licorice flavor common in many savory Asian dishes.

SUMAC POWDER

The dried and crushed berries of the sumac bush that grows wild in all Mediterranean areas. The purple-red powder has a tart, fruity flavor and is most commonly used in dishes from Lebanon, Syria, Turkey and Iran in place of fresh lemon.

ZA'ATAR

Also known as zahtar, this Middle Eastern and North African seasoning is a blend of roasted thyme, sesame seeds and ground sumac.

The Paisley Palate Cookbook

COOKING UNDER PRESSURE

I am not a big proponent of filling your kitchen with a bunch of trivial cooking equipment. Who really needs a melon baller or asparagus peeler? You can turn out some top-notch meals with little more than a quality stockpot, skillet and sharp knife at your disposal, but as I incorporate more whole foods into my lifestyle, I find myself turning time and time again to the pressure cooker as an invaluable piece of equipment. It makes short work of otherwise time intensive foods like beans, lentils and whole grains thus making healthy, flavorful, real food accessible in minutes while saving energy and money in the process.

The secret to the pressure cooker's speed boils down to the laws of physics. The temperature of water in an open pot can never exceed the boiling point because it simply evaporates off in the form of steam. A sealed pressure cooker, on the other hand, prevents the steam from escaping thereby increasing the pressure on the water, which increases its boiling point and tah-dah, slashes cooking times by up to 70 percent. Of course less time spent cooking means less wasted energy, about two-thirds less energy to be exact, and that translates to money in your pocket.

Granted, the conservation of time, energy and money are appealing arguments for the pressure cooker, but I consent to the fact that no equipment is worth its weight in salt if you don't enjoy eating what comes out of it. In this regard, I have found that the sealed cooking environment of a pressure cooker allows for the infusion of flavor into the food resulting in an end product to rival those produced by slow cooking methods. Plus, the capturing of cooking liquid within the pot means more vitamins and minerals are retained than with boiling or even steaming methods and the lack of air exposure prevents oxidation of these nutrients.

It is for these reasons that I use a pressure cooker to prepare many of the recipes included in this book. Though certainly not a kitchen necessity, it is worth consideration as a small investment with numerous culinary rewards. There are many quality books and websites that can assist you in identifying the pressure cooker that is best for you as well as discovering, or rediscovering, the wonderful world of pressure cooking. One of my favorite sites is www.hippressurecooking.com.

This being said, the lack of a pressure cooker should not prevent you from enjoying a single one of the dishes in the pages that follow. A comprehensive cooking time chart for dried beans, lentils, dal and grains can be found on page 189. This can be used to help you swap out cooking methods as well as ingredient varieties.

WHEN USING A PRESSURE COOKER, ALWAYS READ AND FOLLOW THE SAFETY GUIDELINES PROVIDED BY THE MANUFACTURE

The Paisley Palate Cookbook

Opposite page: A local girl helps prepares lunch in the kitchen of the Yoga Vidya Dham Ashram in Trimbek, India.

SOUPS

VEGETABLE STOCK

makes 2½ quarts

I know that store bought stock has come a long way since those devious little desiccated cubes, but homemade vegetable stock is a snap. Plus, there's something to be said for the smell of rich broth simmering on the stove and filling the house with its comforting aroma. I have a serious love affair with soup so I make a batch of this just about every other week in the cooler months. What I don't use immediately, I store in 2-3 cup portions in the freezer.

Prep Time: 15 minutes
Cook Time: 1 hour
Vegan, Gluten Free

3 quarts	water
1	medium onion, peeled and quartered
3	medium carrots, peeled and quartered crosswise
6 ribs	celery, trimmed and quartered crosswise
3 cloves	garlic, peeled
2	leeks, green and white parts, trimmed, halved lengthwise and quartered crosswise
1	medium tomato, quartered
2 ounces	fresh parsley, leaves and stems (about 1½ cup loosely packed)
3 sprigs	fresh thyme (or 1 teaspoon dried)
1 teaspoon	whole black peppercorns
2	bay leaves
2 teaspoons	sea salt (optional)

Combine all the ingredients in a large, heavy bottomed stockpot over high heat. Bring to a boil. Reduce the heat to medium-low and simmer partially covered until the stock is reduced to 2½ quarts or up to 45 minutes (whichever occurs first).

Pour the stock into a second container through a strainer lined with muslin or cheesecloth. Press the vegetables with a wooden spoon to extract as much stock as possible. The stock is ready to use immediately.

Any stock you wish to store for later use can be refrigerated for 3-4 days or frozen for up to 2 months.

Refrain from simmering the stock for more than 45 minutes. In that time, the vegetables give up all their flavors to the water. Simmering them longer will only turn the vegetables into mush and cause the flavors to dull.

TALUMEIN SOUP

makes 1½ quarts

This soup is offered at many Chinese restaurants. With more vegetables and noodles than is traditional, this variation can fill a bowl with more than enough comforting flavor and substance to stand on its own. Don't let the long list of ingredients fool you-this is a simple soup. The small amount of prep time is mostly dedicated to slicing vegetables in an artful manner, really quite a relaxing and therapeutic task if you allow it to be.

Prep Time: 15 minutes
Cook Time: 20 minutes
Vegan

2 tablespoons	vegetable oil
¼ cup	peas
2-3	baby corn, quartered lengthwise
2 florets	broccoli, sliced lengthwise ¼-inch thick
⅓ cup	mushrooms, sliced lengthwise ¼-inch thick
½	small carrot, peeled and cut into ¼-inch thick discs
2 florets	cauliflower, sliced lengthwise ¼-inch thick
⅓ cup	green beans, trimmed and cut into 1-inch lengths
½ cup	cabbage, thinly sliced
1	small green onion, green and white parts, thinly sliced (reserve most of the green parts for garnish)
6 cups	vegetable stock
2 tablespoons	soy sauce
½ teaspoon	black pepper powder
¼ cup	corn starch combined with ¼ cup cool water
¾ cup	wheat noodles, such as Hakka, cooked

Corn starch is used as a traditional thickening agent in this recipe and can be substituted with ½ cup white flour or 3 tablespoons arrowroot powder. With either alternative, follow the same procedure of mixing with enough cool water to make a smooth, thin paste before adding it to the soup.

Combine the corn starch and cool water. Mix together to form a smooth, thin paste. Set aside for later.

Pour the oil into a large pot over high heat. Once the oil is hot, add the vegetables and stir-fry for 3 minutes. Add the vegetable stock, soy sauce and pepper. Bring to a boil then reduce heat to low and simmer for 10 minutes uncovered.

If the water has separated from the corn starch, stir the mixture to re-form a thin paste consistency. Gently stir the soup while adding the corn starch mixture. Continue to gently stir until the soup thickens, 1-2 minutes. Stir in the noodles and heat through. Salt to taste.

Portion the soup into serving bowls, garnish with reserved onion greens and serve hot.

Traditional accompaniments for talumein soup include chilies in vinegar and chili sauce. To make chilies in vinegar, add 3-4 thinly sliced green chilies to ½ cup white vinegar.

Find a recipe for basic chili sauce on p.134.

PEA AND CARROT SOUP

makes 1 quart

Our houseman Jeet, who took such good care of my husband and I while we were living in India, prepared this for us one chilly winter night. After nearly licking our bowls clean I went to Jeet, pen and notebook in hand, asking for the recipe. Well, I definitely did not need that pen or notebook because this is a brilliantly, almost shamefully, simple soup. Its short list of ingredients is a testament to the "less is more" philosophy. Its clean flavors serve as my sentimental reminder to stop complicating things. This recipe now serves as my base formula for an unlimited repertoire of purée soups, a couple of my other favorites I've also included in this section.

Prep Time: 10 minutes
Cook Time: 30 minutes
Vegan, Gluten Free

3 tablespoons	olive oil
3	small red onion, sliced into thin strips
1 cup	fresh, shelled peas
2	medium carrots, chopped
3 cups	vegetable broth
(1 teaspoon)	salt
(¼ teaspoon)	black pepper powder

Pour the oil into a large pot over medium heat. Once the oil is hot, add the onion and cook until tender and nicely browned, about 8-10 minutes. Add the carrots and peas and continue to cook 10 more minutes, stirring regularly. Add the vegetable stock and bring to a boil. Reduce the heat, cover and simmer for 5 minutes. Then remove the pot from the heat and allow the mixture to cool slightly.

Transfer mixture to a blender and blend until smooth. Transfer back into the pot and gently reheat, leaving it on the heat until the desired consistency is reached. Season to taste with salt and pepper.

Ladle the soup into serving bowls and serve hot.

SOUTH INDIAN SAMBAR

makes 1 quart

Sambar can be described as a lentil based curry or vegetable stew. Both spicy and sour, it is the ever-present accompaniment of all dishes south Indian, be it breakfast lunch or dinner.

Prep Time: 15 minutes
Cook Time: 35 minutes
Vegan, Gluten Free

Sambar powder can be readily found in the ethnic foods aisle or asian market, but you can also make your own. The following recipe makes 1 cup of powder:

½ cup coriander seeds
½ cup dried red chilies
½ tsp. fenugreek seeds
1 tsp. black peppercorns
1 tsp. cumin seeds
¼ tsp. mustard seeds
1 T. besan flour
1 tsp. turmeric powder
⅛ tsp. asafoetida

Warm a skillet over medium heat. Dry roast all but the last 3 ingredients until aromatic then allow them to cool. In a spice/coffee grinder, grind together all ingredients to form a coarse powder. Cool. Store in an airtight container.

⅓ cup	dried toor dal
½ teaspoon	turmeric powder
2 tablespoons	oil
½ teaspoon	cumin seeds
¼ teaspoon	mustard seeds
⅛ teaspoon	fenugreek seeds
⅛ teaspoon	asafoetida powder
4	whole dried red chilies
12	curry leaves
3	small tomatoes, large chopped
2 cups	mixed vegetables such as carrot, cauliflower, green beans, squash, potato, drumstick, medium chopped
1 teaspoon	salt
1 tablespoon	sambar powder
2 tablespoons	dried mango powder
(½ teaspoon)	salt

Rinse the dal and remove any stones. Place the dal in the pressure cooker along with the turmeric and 2½ cups water. Secure the lid on the cooker and place over high heat. Once the cooker builds enough pressure to release one whistle, reduce the heat to low and continue to cook for an additional 7 minutes. Remove the pressure cooker from the heat and allow the pressure to dissipate fully before opening.

Heat the oil in a large skillet over medium heat. When the oil is hot add the cumin seeds, mustard seeds, fenugreek seeds, asafetida, chilies and curry leaves and cook until the seeds begin to sputter, about 20 seconds. Stir in the tomatoes, mixed vegetables and the teaspoon of salt. Cover and cook until the vegetables are just tender and cooked through, about 10 minutes, stirring occasionally. Stir in the sambar powder, mango powder and about 1 cup of water. Bring the mixture to a boil then reduce the heat to low, cover and simmer for 3 minutes.

Stir the vegetable mixture into to the cooked dal. With the pressure cooker lid off, bring to a boil then reduce the heat to low, and simmer for 10 minutes.

Transfer the sambar to a serving dish. Serve hot along side your favorite south Indian dish.

ROASTED BEETROOT
AND GARLIC SOUP

makes 1¼ quart

This recipe is adapted from one sent to me by my foodie friend Jeremy who found the original in Whole Living magazine. It's a beautiful and delicious soup that happens to come with a laundry list of health benefits. When handling beets, some people like to wear gloves to protect their hands from being stained, but I say that's nonsense. Wear your beet stained fingers as a badge of honor. After all, you're cooking real food for your loved ones. You're a modern day hero!

Prep Time: 15 minutes
Cook Time: 1 hour 30 minutes
Gluten Free

1 bulb	garlic
1 pound	beetroot (about 3 medium beets)
2 tablespoons	olive oil, plus more for roasting
1	leek, white and some green parts thinly sliced
2 sprigs	fresh thyme leaves, finely chopped
	(or ½ teaspoon dried)
3 cups	vegetable stock
1 tablespoon	lime juice
(1 teaspoon)	salt
(¼ teaspoon)	black pepper powder
¼ cup	sour cream or yogurt for garnish

Preheat the oven to 425°F/218°C.

One bulb of garlic may sound like a lot, but roasting transforms the garlic's sharp bite into a mild, sweet and buttery flavor.

Trim the tip of the garlic bulb ¼ inch to just expose the tops of the garlic cloves themselves. Place the bulb on a sheet of aluminum foil, drizzle with olive oil and seal the foil into a loose pouch around the bulb. Likewise, drizzle the beets with olive oil and seal them into their own foil pouch. Place both pouches in the oven and roast them until the garlic cloves are soft and creamy and the beets are fork-tender throughout. This will take about 1 hour for medium sized beets. Allow them to cool unwrapped until they can be easily handled. Squeeze the garlic cloves out of their paper skins and set the cloves aside. Peel the beets and cut them into 1-inch pieces.

Pour 2 tablespoons of olive oil into a large pan over medium heat. Once the oil is hot, add the leek and cook until tender, about 6 minutes. Add the garlic, beets, thyme and stock. Bring to a boil then reduce the heat, cover and

simmer for 5 minutes. Remove the pot from the heat and allow the mixture to cool slightly.

Transfer mixture to a blender and blend until smooth. Transfer back into the pot and gently reheat, leaving it on the heat until the desired consistency is reached. Stir in the lime juice and season to taste with salt and pepper.

Ladle the soup into serving bowls and serve hot with a dollop of sour cream or yogurt as a garnish.

Make Roasted Pumpkin and Garlic Soup by substituting pumpkin for the beets. The pumpkin can be roasted without being wrapped in foil.

SPROUTED MUNG BEAN SOUP

makes 2 quarts

Supercharged. That's how I feel when I eat this soup. Sprouting beans is a great way to turn long shelf life staples into live foods that offer loads of health benefits. This soup is ideal for winter when much of our fresh food may be brought in from far away. It provides that much needed shot of vitality when the body is seeking a little reassurance that spring is indeed coming.

Prep Time: 10 minutes
Cook Time: 20 minutes
Vegan, Gluten Free

3 cups	sprouted mung beans
1 tablespoon	oil
1½ teaspoon	mustard seeds
1 tablespoon	cumin seeds
½ teaspoon	turmeric powder
⅛ teaspoon	asafetida powder
1¾ pound	tomatoes, chopped (about 5 cups prepared)
1 tablespoon	ginger, minced or micro-planed
(2 teaspoons)	salt

To sprout your own mung beans, begin by soaking half the desired quantity in fresh water overnight. The next morning, drain and rinse the beans. Leave them in an inverted mason jar fitted with a screen lid, muslin or cheesecloth. Rinse and drain the beans a minimum of 4 times throughout the course of the day. The beans will sprout and be ready to use by the end of the day. For longer sprouts, continue the process for 1-2 additional days.

Rinse the sprouted mung beans then place them in a pressure cooker along with 5 cups of water. Secure the lid on the cooker and place it over high heat. Once the cooker builds enough pressure to release one whistle, reduce the heat to low and continue to cook the beans for 5 additional minutes. Remove the cooker from the heat and allow the pressure to dissipate fully before opening.

Pour the oil into a medium saucepan over medium heat. When the oil is hot, add the cumin and mustard seeds and cook until they begin to sputter, about 20 seconds. Add the turmeric and asafetida and cook another 30 seconds. Stir in the tomatoes and ginger and cook for 2 minutes then add the tomato-spice mixture to the cooked mung beans. Increase the heat to high and bring to a boil. Reduce the heat, cover (with flat lid, not sealed pressure cooker lid) and simmer for 10 minutes.

I like a thicker soup so at this point I transfer half the soup to a blender, purée it and stir it back into the rest of the soup in the pressure cooker pot. But you can assess the thickness of your soup and omit this step if you prefer.

Season to taste with salt.

Ladle the soup into bowls and serve hot.

The nutritional content of sprouted beans and seeds is many times greater than that from which it sprouts. As a seed or bean sprouts, it produces additional vitamins, anti-oxidants and enzymes.

SWEET POTATO-LEEK SOUP

makes 1½ quarts

Autumn, just about the time Delhi begins to make sincere promise of cooler weather, sweet potato vendors can be found preparing tapas sized portions of Shakarkandi. These chunks of roasted yellow sweet potato drizzled with lime and sprinkled with a chaat masala gave me the idea for this soup. Use any type of sweet potato you prefer. There are an incredible number of varieties to choose from. They range in color from deep violet to light yellow and each offers a unique sweetness.

Prep Time: 20 minutes
Cook Time: 40 minutes
Gluten Free

2 tablespoons	oil
1 pound	sweet potatoes, peeled and chopped
	(about 2 medium potatoes or 2 cups prepared)
2	leeks, white and some green parts thinly sliced
4 cups	vegetable stock, divided
2 teaspoons	chaat masala
(½ teaspoon)	salt
(¼ teaspoon)	black pepper powder
(2 teaspoons)	lime juice
½ cup	sour cream or yogurt, for garnish

Chaat Masala is a special blend of spices available at most asian markets. Its combination of both sweet and sour tastes is designed especially for street snacks such as Bhelpuri, Golgappa, Aloo Chaat and Dahi puri and often contains chili powder, cumin seed, coriander, dried mango powder, black salt, sea salt, ginger powder, and bay leaf.

Pour the oil into a large pot over medium heat. Once the oil is hot, add the leeks and cook until tender and slightly browned, about 8-10 minutes. Add the potatoes and continue to cook 10 more minutes, stirring regularly. Stir in the chaat masala. Add the vegetable stock and bring to a boil. Reduce the heat, cover and simmer until the potatoes are tender, about 10-15 minutes. Then remove the pot from the heat and allow the mixture to cool slightly.

Transfer to mixture to a blender and blend until smooth. Return the soup to the pot. Gently reheat the soup, leaving it on the heat until desired consistency is reached. Season to taste with salt, pepper and lime juice.

Ladle the soup into serving bowls and serve hot with a dollop of sour cream or yogurt as a garnish.

SPICY CARROT SOUP

makes 1½ quarts

Sometimes I don't know if I like eating or looking at this soup more. Carrots prodded along by paprika and red chili give rise to this soup's fiery orange color and vibrant spiciness. This soup is a beautiful melding of the fresh, bright flavors of the Mediterranean with the warm earthy flavors of the Middle East. A dollop of coriander yogurt helps to balance the spice and add a hint of creaminess.

Prep Time: 15 minutes
Cook Time: 45 minutes
Gluten Free

2 tablespoons	olive oil
1	medium onion, sliced into thin strips
1 pound	carrots, peeled and chopped
	(about 4 medium carrots or 2 cups prepared)
1	bay leaf
1 teaspoon	cumin powder
1 teaspoon	coriander powder
1 teaspoon	red chili powder
2 teaspoons	paprika powder
4 cups	vegetable stock
(1½ teaspoon)	salt
(¼ teaspoon)	black pepper powder
1 cup	yogurt
¼ cup	fresh coriander, chopped

Pour the oil into a large pot over medium heat. Once the oil is hot, add the onion and carrot and cook until both are nicely browned, about 8-10 minutes. Add the bay leaf and spices and cook for another 1 minute. Add the vegetable stock and bring to a boil. Reduce the heat and simmer uncovered until the carrot is tender, about 10 minutes.

Remove the pot from the heat and allow the soup to cool slightly then transfer to a blender and blend until smooth. A full batch of soup will require multiple batches in the blender. Return the soup to the pot and gently reheat. Season to taste with salt and pepper.

In a small bowl, combine the yogurt and the fresh coriander.

Portion the soup into serving bowls and serve hot with a dollop of coriander-yogurt on top and additional on the side.

LENTIL AND GREENS SOUP

makes 1½ quarts

I admit that I used to be among the many who believe lentil soups are best left to retirement homes and tired diners, but preparation is everything. This soup is fresh and bright and one of the reasons I now maintain a lucid love for lentils.

Prep Time: 20 minutes
Cook Time: 40 minutes
Vegan, Gluten Free

1 cup	dried brown/green lentils
2 tablespoons	olive oil
1	large onion
3 cloves	garlic, peeled and crushed
4 cups	vegetable stock
1 pound	fresh greens such as fenugreek or chard, washed and trimmed (about 12 cups loosely packed)
½ cup	fresh coriander, chopped
3 tablespoons	fresh lemon or lime juice

Rinse the lentils and remove any stones. Place them in a pressure cooker along with 4½ cups of water. Secure the lid on the cooker and place it over high heat. Once the cooker builds enough pressure to release one whistle, reduce the heat to low and continue to cook the lentils for 9 additional minutes. Remove the cooker from the heat and allow the pressure to dissipate fully before opening.

Pour the oil into a large size pot over medium heat. Once the oil is hot, add the onion and cook until tender and slightly browned, about 8-10 minutes. Add the garlic and cook for 1 additional minute. Add the greens and cook until wilted, about 3 minutes. Add the vegetable stock and lentils and bring to a boil. Reduce the heat, cover and simmer for 10 minutes. Stir in the coriander and lemon or lime juice.

For a thicker soup, blend 2 cups of the vegetable broth with half of the cooked lentils prior to adding them to the greens.

Portion the soup into serving bowls and serve hot.

THUKPA

makes 2 quarts

Thukpa is a noodle soup that is Tibetan in origin but well known throughout all the Himalayan countries. Usually a clear broth soup, much like an unthickened variation of Talumein Soup (p.13), this variation carries more of an Indian influence using masoor dal (red dal) to create a more substantial consistency that makes it an ideal one-bowl meal. The hand rolled noodles are regionally traditional and simple to make, but I've also enjoyed this version of thukpa sans noodles atop a generous bed of rice.

Prep Time: 25 minutes
Cook Time: 50 minutes
Vegan

FOR THE SOUP

1 cup	dried masoor dal
3 tablespoons	oil
2	small onion, chopped
2 tablespoons	ginger, minced or micro-planed
4 cloves	garlic, minced or micro-planed
1	green chili, trimmed, seeded and minced (optional)
1 teaspoon	coriander powder
½ teaspoon	turmeric powder
6 cups	mixed vegetables such as tomato, carrot, cauliflower, green beans, squash, potato, chopped
½ teaspoon	garam masala powder
(2 teaspoons)	salt
½ cup	fresh coriander, chopped

FOR THE NOODLES

½ cups (2.6 oz.)	atta
¼ teaspoon	salt
¾ tablespoon	vegetable oil
±¼ cup	water

Rinse the dal and remove any stones. Place the dal in a pressure cooker along with 5 cups water. Secure the lid on the cooker and place it over high heat. Once the cooker builds enough pressure to release one whistle, reduce the heat to low and continue to cook for an additional 5 minutes. Remove the cooker from the heat and allow the pressure to dissipate fully before opening.

Pour the oil into a large wok or skillet over medium heat. Once the oil is hot, add the onion and cook until tender, about 5 minutes. Add the garlic, ginger and green chili and cook for 30 seconds. Stir in the coriander and turmeric powders and cook for another 30 seconds. Add the vegetables and cook until just tender, about 10 minutes stirring regularly.

Stir the vegetables into the cooked dal, bring to a boil then reduce the heat to low, cover (with flat lid, not sealed pressure cooker lid) and simmer 20 minutes.

While the soup simmers, prepare the noodles. In a small bowl, combine the flour, salt and oil. Using your hand to incorporate, add about 2 tablespoons of water. Continue to add water in tiny increments until a tacky textured dough ball forms. Turn the dough out onto a clean, lightly floured surface and knead until the dough becomes smooth and elastic, about 5 minutes. Pinch off a piece of dough about the size of a small marble (approximately ½-inch in diameter). Roll it between well-floured hands into a smooth round ball. Then place the dough ball on the counter and roll it back and forth along the length of your palm to form a noodle shape about 3 inches in length with tapered ends. Set it aside and repeat this process until all the remaining dough is used.

Lightly tossing your hand rolled noodles in a little additional atta will prevent them from sticking to one another while they await cooking.

Stir the noodles into the simmering soup and cook through, about 6 minutes. Stir in the garam masala. Season to taste with salt then stir in the fresh coriander.

Ladle the thukpa into bowls. Serve hot with Hari Chutney (p.135) or Laal Chutney (p.136) on the side.

MUSHROOM SOUP

makes 1 quart

I've always loved mushrooms, any and all kinds. When I was younger, my mom once purchased a case of portabellas from one of those bulk warehouse stores. It was a small act that seemed to seal the entire family into a fungus focused foods biosphere for the better part of two weeks. Even after what my family still refers to as the portabella over dose incident, I continue to love mushrooms. This recipe could not be more basic and yet the rich earthy flavor consistently blows me away.

Prep Time: 10 minutes
Cook Time: 35 minutes
Vegan, Gluten Free

2 tablespoons	olive oil
2	medium onions, sliced into thin strips
3 cups	mushrooms, any variety, sliced
3 cups	vegetable stock
(1 teaspoon)	salt
(¼ teaspoon)	black pepper powder

Pour the oil into a large pot over medium heat. Once the oil is hot, add the onion and cook until tender and nicely browned, about 8-10 minutes. Add the mushrooms and continue to cook until they are also nicely browned, about 10 more minutes, stirring regularly. Add the vegetable stock and bring to a boil. Reduce the heat, cover and simmer for 10 minutes. Then remove the pot from the heat and allow the mixture to cool slightly.

Transfer mixture to a blender and blend until smooth. Transfer back into the pot and gently reheat, leaving it on the heat until the desired consistency is reached. Season to taste with salt and pepper.

Ladle the soup into serving bowls and serve hot.

CURRIED SQUASH AND APPLE SOUP

makes 2½ quarts

In her book 'Parties', Ina Garten has a recipe for Butternut Squash and Apple Soup, which she adapted from Julee Rosso and Sheila Lukins's book The Silver Palate. The page of my copy of Ina's book containing the recipe for this sweet little soup with the rich orange color is happily adorned with splatter from the numerous batches I've made over the years. Written in my handwriting across the top of the page is one word, 'Fantastic!' My version was adapted from Ina's recipe and is my absolute all-time favorite fall soup.

Prep Time: 20 minutes
Cook Time: 40 minutes
Vegan, Gluten Free

3 tablespoons	olive oil
2 cups	onions, chopped
2 tablespoons	curry powder
3 pounds	sweet squash flesh, such as pumpkin, butternut or banana squash, cut into medium chunks
1 pound	sweet apples, peeled, quartered and cored (about 3-4 medium apples or 2 cups prepared)
1 cup	apple juice or cider
1 teaspoon	cinnamon powder
(1 teaspoon)	salt
(1 teaspoon)	black pepper powder

Any store bought curry powder will work fine, or you can blend your own. The following is a formula for a basic curry powder:

8 parts cumin powder
7 parts coriander powder
2 parts ginger powder
4 parts turmeric powder
.5 part red chili powder

Pour the oil into the pot of a pressure cooker over a medium heat. Once the oil is hot, add the onion and cook until onions are tender, about 15 minutes, stirring frequently. Add the curry powder and cook for another 3 minutes. Add 3 cups water and scrape the bottom of the pot with a wooden spoon to release any catchings.

Add the squash, apples, cinnamon, salt and pepper. Secure the lid on the cooker and increase the heat to high. Once the cooker builds enough pressure to release one whistle, reduce the heat to low and continue to cook for an additional 3 minutes. Remove the cooker from the heat and allow the pressure to dissipate fully before opening.

Allow the squash mixture to cool slightly then transfer to a blender and blend until smooth. A full batch of soup will require multiple blender batches.

Return the soup to the cooker pot and stir in the apple juice or cider. Gently reheat the soup, leaving it on the heat until desired consistency is reached.

Adjust the seasonings to taste.

Ladle the soup into bowls and serve hot.

TOMATO SOUP

makes 1 quart

Truth be known, the thing I like most about tomato soup is that its mere presence suggests a crispy, melty, grilled cheese sandwich is not too far away. Combinations like this are considered classics for a reason. It is tried and true, honest food for the honest man. It doesn't get much more straightforward than a grilled cheese's tomato soup dunk on its way to your mouth and the very least we can do is give the grilled cheese something worth its wading time.

Prep Time: 15 minute
Cook Time: 45 minutes
Vegan, Gluten Free

3 tablespoon	olive oil
1	medium onion, sliced into thin strips
2 pounds	tomatoes
	(about 12 of a medium variety such as Roma)
2	medium carrots, peeled and chopped
1 rib	celery, chopped
3-4 cloves	garlic, smashed
2 tablespoons	ginger, chopped
1	bay leaf
3 cups	vegetable stock
(1½ teaspoon)	salt
(¼ teaspoon)	black pepper powder

Place the tomatoes in a saucepan with enough water to cover the tomatoes by one inch. Place the pan over high heat and bring to a boil. Continue to boil the tomatoes for 10 minutes. Remove the tomatoes from the water, cut them in quarters and set them aside.

Pour 2 tablespoons of the oil into a large pot over medium heat. Once the oil is hot, add the onion and cook until tender and nicely browned, about 8-10 minutes. Add the tomatoes, carrot, celery, garlic, ginger, and bay leaf and continue to cook 5 more minutes. Pour in the vegetable stock and bring to a boil. Reduce the heat to low and simmer partially covered for 30 minutes. Remove the pot from the heat and allow the soup to cool slightly.

Remove the bay leaf, transfer the soup to a blender and blend until smooth, adding 1 tablespoon of oil while the blender is running. Transfer the soup back into the pot through a fine mesh strainer. Gently reheat the soup, leaving it on the heat until desired consistency is reached. Season to taste with salt and pepper.

Serve hot with croutons, toast points…or my favorite, grilled cheese sandwiches.

COLD CUCUMBER-ALMOND SOUP

makes 1 quart

This is an awesome warm weather soup, not only because it's a cold soup, but because the cucumber and fresh herbs help to replenish much of what the heat takes out of you in terms of water and minerals. It's easy to make and only gets better if you can let it sit for some time.

Prep Time: 15 minutes + 4 hours chill time recommended
Cook Time: 10 minutes
Gluten Free

½ cup	blanched almonds
1	large cucumber, peeled and seeded
1¾ cups	yogurt
1¼ cups	milk or buttermilk
¼ cup	flat leaf parsley, finely chopped
1 clove	garlic, minced or micro-planed
2 tablespoons	fresh chives, finely chopped (or 2 teaspoons dried)
2 tablespoons	fresh dill, finely chopped (or 2 teaspoons dried)
(½ teaspoon)	salt

Preheat an oven to 325°F/163°C.

Place the almonds on a baking sheet and toast them until lightly browned, about 10-15 minutes, shaking the sheet frequently. Remove from the oven and set aside to cool. Once cooled, coarsely chop the almonds. Separate out 1 tablespoon to be used as a garnish.

For instructions for blanching your own almonds refer to the side note on p. 153.

Coarsely chop ¾ of the cucumber then purée it in a food processor. Chop the remaining ¼ cucumber into small dice. In a bowl, combine the cucumber purée and pieces, yogurt, milk, garlic, herbs and almonds. Stir to evenly distribute all the ingredients. Season to taste with salt. Cover the soup and refrigerate. Though delicious immediately, this soup is best when allowed to refrigerated for 4 hours.

Serve cold, garnished with reserved chopped almonds and a scattering of any remaining herbs.

Opposite page: Fresh vegetables displayed for sale at Pike Place Market in Seattle, Washington, U.S.A.

SALADS

FATTOUSH SALAD

makes 2 mains/4-6 sides

My sister and I always joke that we don't take good pictures because our beauty is fluid. That is to say that it can't be captured in a single still shot and is best appreciated in the reality of the moment. Fattoush salad was born of a similar attitude. An ingredient list for this authentic Lebanese peasant salad is difficult to nail down because farmers include whatever is in season at the moment.

Prep Time: 20 minutes
Cook Time: 10 minutes

FOR THE SALAD

2	pita bread rounds
6	Romaine lettuce leaves, shredded
2	medium cucumbers, peeled, seeded and cut into ½-inch cubes
4	tomatoes of a medium variety such as Roma, cut into ½-inch cubes
4	green onions, white and green parts thinly sliced
¼ cup	fresh parsley, chopped
20	fresh mint leaves, finely chopped
¼ cup	fresh coriander, chopped
1 tablespoon	sumac powder
	salt
	pepper

FOR THE DRESSING

2 cloves	garlic, minced or micro-planed
3 ounces	feta cheese
¼ cup	olive oil
¼ cup	lemon juice
¼ teaspoon	sugar

Preheat the oven to 350°F/176°C.

Bake the pita bread rounds on a baking sheet in the oven until they are golden brown and crisp, about 3-4 minutes on each side. When they are cool enough to handle, break them into pieces and set them aside.

For the dressing, place the garlic, feta and most of the olive oil in a small bowl. Use the back of a fork to smash the feta against the side of the bowl

and work it into a relatively smooth mixture. Mix in the remainder of the oil, lemon juice, sugar and sumac.

In a large bowl, combine the vegetables and herbs. Pour in the dressing and toss to coat. Season to taste with salt and pepper. Add in the pita pieces, toss again and serve promptly.

LENTIL SALAD

makes 2 mains/4-6 sides

Much like Spanish tapas, the mezze of the Middle East is a spread of simple yet delicious dishes. Whether the spread itself is minimal or elaborate, the tradition represents the pleasure of savoring small bites in good company.

Versions of this salad can be found throughout North Africa and the Middle East. It makes a nice offering as part of a mezze, but can also make a satisfying meal all on its own. Consider using Puy lentils if they are available to you as they hold their shape nicely and add a touch of peppery flavor.

Prep Time: 15 minutes + 30 minutes sitting time recommended
Cook Time: 15 minutes
Vegan, Gluten Free

FOR THE SALAD

1 cup	dried brown or green lentils
1	medium onion
3 cloves	garlic, peeled
1	bay leaf
1 teaspoons	cumin powder

FOR THE DRESSING

2 tablespoons	red wine vinegar
1 tablespoon	lime juice
¼ cup	olive oil
1 teaspoon	cumin powder
3	green onions, white and green parts thinly sliced
¼ cup	fresh coriander, chopped
1¼ teaspoon	salt
¼ teaspoon	black pepper powder

Rinse the lentils and remove any stones. Place the lentils in a pressure cooker. Peel the onion leaving the ends in tact. Stud the onion with the cloves and place the onion in the cooker along with the garlic, bay leaf, cumin powder and 3 cups water. Secure the lid on the cooker and place the cooker over high heat. Allow the cooker to build enough pressure to release one whistle then lower the heat to low and continue to cook for 9 more minutes. Remove the cooker from the heat and allow the pressure to dissipate fully before opening.

In a large bowl, prepare the dressing. Whisk together the vinegar, lime juice, oil, cumin powder, spring onions, coriander, salt and pepper.

Drain the cooked lentils and remove the onion and bay leaf. Pour the warm
lentils directly into the bowl of dressing and stir to coat the lentils completely.
If time allows, cover, and let the salad to sit for 20-30 minutes so the flavors
can meld.

Serve warm or room temperature.

BEETROOT AND TOMATO SALAD

makes 2 mains/4-6 sides

Tadka is the process of tempering spices in hot oil in order to enhance their flavor.

This salad comes from the kitchen of the Yoga Vidya Dam Ashram in Trimbek, India. It is one of the most popular salads they serve. The same tadka preparation can be used for many different variations, some of which I've included.

Prep Time: 15 minutes
Cook Time: 30 minutes
Vegan, Gluten Free

1 pound	beetroot, washed and trimmed
	(about 2-3 medium beets or 2 cups prepared)
1 tablespoon	oil
1 teaspoon	mustard seeds
1 teaspoon	cumin seeds
¼ teaspoon	turmeric powder
⅛ teaspoon	asafoetida powder
1 teaspoon	salt
1½ teaspoon	sugar
2 cups	tomatoes, chopped
	(about 4 of a medium variety such as Roma)
1 tablespoon	lime juice
¾ cup	roasted peanut powder
½ cup	fresh coriander, chopped

Place the beets in a large pot and generously cover them with water. Place the pot over high heat and bring to a boil. Reduce the heat, cover and simmer until the beets are tender enough to be easily pierced with a knife (about 30 minutes for medium sized beets). If your beets vary greatly in size, you may need to remove the smaller ones earlier. Drain the beets and set aside to cool. Once the beets are cool enough to handle, slip the skins off with your fingers and chop them into ¼-inch cubes.

As an alternative to boiling, you can roast the beets. To do this, drizzle the beets with olive oil and loosely wrap them in aluminum foil. Roast them in a 400°F/205°C oven for roughly 1 hour.

Pour the oil into a small saucepan over medium heat. When the oil is hot, add the mustard seeds and cook until they begin to sputter, about 20 seconds. Add the cumin seeds, turmeric, asafetida and salt and cook another 30 seconds. Remove the temper mixture from the heat and stir in the sugar.

In a large bowl, combine the beets and tomatoes. Add the temper mixture and lime juice and stir to coat evenly. Stir in the peanut powder and coriander. Adjust the salt and sugar if needed.

Serve chilled or room temperature.

VARIATIONS

If you are lucky enough to get fresh beets with the green tops still attached and vibrant, keep them. You can cook and eat these like any other slightly bitter green.

Carrot and Pomegranate Salad:
>In place of beet and tomato, add
>>2½ cups raw carrot, peeled and grated
>>1½ cup pomegranate seeds

Cucumber Salad:
>In place of beet and tomato, add
>>4 cups raw cucumber, peeled seeded and chopped

WARM GARBANZO BEAN
AND CHARD SALAD

makes 2 mains/4-6 sides

Chard is often confused with spinach, though the large, dark green leaves of chard contain deep crinkles and sit atop thick stems that come in a rainbow variety of colors. Chard is essentially a hearty beet green minus the beet at the end so one can be substituted for the other provided the cooking time is shortened for the more delicate beet greens.

Chard is one of those multi-century old vegetables that are now presented under the category of super food. It's a robust leafy green that has long been used in Mediterranean and Middle Eastern cooking. Combined with the beloved garbanzo bean and a few spices, I begin to wonder who's behind the eating healthy is confusing conspiracy anyway?

Prep Time: 20 minutes + 8 hours soaking time for the beans
Cook Time: 25 minutes
Vegan, Gluten Free

1 cup	dried garbanzo beans (about 2 cups cooked)
¼ cup	olive oil
1	medium onion, sliced into strips
2	medium tomatoes, seeded and chopped small
1 teaspoon	sugar
½ teaspoon	cinnamon powder
1 clove	garlic, minced or micro-planed
3 pounds	chard, washed, trimmed and cut into ½-inch strips
¼ cup	fresh mint leaves, chopped
2 tablespoons	lemon juice
2 tablespoons	sumac
(¼ teaspoon)	salt

Rinse the beans and remove any stones. Cover the beans with 6 cups room temperature water and leave to soak for at least 8 hours.

After the beans have been sufficiently soaked, drain and rinse them under running water. Place the beans in a pressure cooker along with 5 cups of water. Secure the lid on the cooker and place it over high heat. Once the cooker builds enough pressure to release one whistle, reduce the heat to low and continue to cook the beans for 13 more minutes. Remove the cooker from the heat and allow the pressure to dissipate fully before opening. Drain the beans and set them aside.

Pour the oil into a large, heavy based frying pan over low heat. Once the oil is warm, add the onion and cook until soft and just browned, about 5-6 minutes. Add the tomato, sugar, cinnamon, garlic and cook for another 2 minutes.

Add the chard and garbanzo beans to the pan and cook just until the chard wilts, about 2-3 minutes. Remove the pan form the heat and stir in the mint, lemon juice, and sumac. Salt to taste.

Transfer the salad to a large dish and serve immediately.

PANZANELLA

makes 2 mains/4-6 sides

The Italians may have invented this salad as a means of using old bread, but great panzanella is a true testament to late summer's tomato perfection. Patience pays when it comes to capturing the elusive flavorful tomato so when great local tomatoes finally come into season, panzanella salad is a great way to celebrate.

Prep Time: 25 minutes + 10 minutes sitting time
Cook Time: 15 minutes
Vegan

FOR THE SALAD

1 pound	1-3 day old rustic bread such as ciabatta, crusts removed and cut into 1-inch cubes (about 3 cups loosely packed prepared cubes)
±3 tablespoons	olive oil
4	medium tomatoes, divided
2	cucumbers, peeled, seeded and chunked
1	small onion, cut in half then thinly sliced
2 tablespoons	capers, rinsed and chopped
2 tablespoons	sun-dried tomatoes, chopped
½ cup	fresh basil leaves, thinly sliced

FOR THE VINAIGRETTE DRESSING

1 clove	garlic, minced or micro-planed
2 tablespoons	red wine vinegar
¼ teaspoon	salt
¼ teaspoon	black pepper powder
¼ cup	olive oil

Position an oven rack approximately 12 inches from the broiler and fire up the broiler.

Place the bread cubes on a large baking sheet, drizzle with olive oil and toss to coat nicely. Place the tray of cubes under the broiler until crisp and just lightly browned, about 8-10 minutes, stirring regularly to promote even toasting.

Alternatively, you can place the oil coated bread cubes in a large skillet, place the skillet on the stove over medium heat and cook until the bread cubes are crisp and just lightly browned, about 4-5 minutes, stirring regularly.

Set the bread cubes aside and allow them to cool while you prepare the rest of the salad.

For the dressing, place 2 of the tomatoes in a small saucepan of water over high heat. Bring to a boil. Continue to boil the tomatoes for 10 minutes. Remove the tomatoes from the water and place them in a blender along with the garlic, vinegar, salt, and pepper. Blend until the tomatoes are fully puréed. With the blender still running, slowly add the olive oil in a thin stream.

Cut each of the 2 remaining tomatoes in half and remove the seeds. Then chop the tomatoes and combine them in a large bowl with the cucumber, onion, capers, sun-dried tomatoes, basil and bread cubes.

Spoon the vinaigrette over the salad and toss to evenly coat. Adjust the seasoning if needed.

Allow the salad to sit for about 10 minutes before serving at room temperature.

TABBOULEH SALAD

makes 6-8 sides

This classic Lebanese salad always makes me think of my friend Taghrid. Each time she visited her family in Lebanon she would return with a cooler filled with produce from her homeland. She said nothing tasted as flavorful as Lebanese produce. I believe her if only because when it comes to Middle Eastern cuisine, the Lebanese are Kings of the kitchen. Their artistic flare, love of fresh food and knowledge of ingredients native to their area are all evident in this fresh, tangy, super-green salad.

Prep Time: 20 minutes + 30 minutes sitting time
Cook Time: 10 minutes
Vegan

2 tablespoons	bulgar wheat
2 tablespoons	fresh lemon juice
2 tablespoons	olive oil
½ teaspoon	salt
3	green onions, white and green parts thinly sliced
2 cups	fresh mint leaves, finely chopped
5 cups	fresh parsley, finely chopped
1	medium cucumber, peeled, seeded and chopped
2 cups	tomatoes, seeded and chopped small (about 4 of a medium variety such as Roma)
¼ teaspoon	Lebanese 7-spice blend (see side note)

Pour ¼ cup water into a medium pot over high heat and bring to a boil. Stir in the bulgar wheat, lemon juice, olive oil, and salt. Cook for 30 seconds then remove from the heat, cover and allow the grain to sit for 30 minutes to absorb the dressing.

In a medium size bowl, combine the green onions, mint, parsley, cucumber and tomatoes and Lebanese 7-spice blend.

Add the dressed bulgar to the herb mixture and stir to combine.

Serve chilled or at room temperature.

Lebanese 7-Spices is a blend of dried, powdered allspice, black pepper, cinnamon, ground clove, nutmeg, fenugreek and ginger in equal proportions. The blend can be found in most Middle Eastern markets, but I simply add a nice pinch of each spice.

GARBANZO BEANS WITH CUMIN DRESSING

makes 2 mains/4-6 sides

This is a salad that was available in almost all delicatessens when I lived in the Middle East. Always freshly made and delicious, I would often eat my entire container standing at the kitchen counter before I could even put my groceries away. Embarrassing, but true.

Prep Time: 20 minutes + 8 hours soaking time for the beans
Cook Time: 15 minutes
Vegan, Gluten Free

1 cup	dried garbanzo beans (about 2 cups cooked)
¼ cup	fresh flat leaf parsley, chopped
1	medium red onion, finely chopped
2 cloves	garlic, minced or micro-planed
¼ cup	lemon
2 tablespoons	olive oil
½ teaspoon	cumin powder
½ teaspoon	red pepper powder
½ teaspoon	salt
½ teaspoon	black pepper powder

Cumin has long been referred to as the "King of Middle Eastern Spices," though it is also an essential flavor in virtually every global cuisine.

Rinse the beans and remove any stones. Cover the beans with 6 cups room temperature water and leave to soak for at least 8 hours.

Drain the beans and rinse them under running water. Place them in a pressure cooker along with 5 cups of water. Secure the lid on the cooker and place it over high heat. Once the cooker builds enough pressure to release one whistle, reduce the heat to low and continue to cook the beans for 13 more minutes. Remove the cooker from the heat and allow the pressure to dissipate fully before opening. Drain the beans and allow them to cool while you prepare the dressing.

In a large bowl whisk together the parsley, onion, garlic, lemon juice, olive oil, cumin powder, red pepper powder, salt and pepper. Add the beans to the dressing and sir to coat.

Serve warm or cold.

GREEK SALAD

makes 2 mains/4-6 sides

There is no secret to great Greek salad, just fresh, crisp produce, quality olives and feta, feta, feta. There's no need for Iceberg lettuce. It only fills the space that could otherwise be filled with feta.

Prep Time: 20 minutes
Cook Time: 0 minutes
Gluten Free

FOR THE SALAD

3	cucumbers, peeled, seeded and chopped
1	green pepper, cut into strips
3	medium tomatoes, cut into wedges
1	small red onion, cut into thin strips
12	Kalamata olives
5 ounces	feta cheese, cubed or roughly crumbled
30 leaves	fresh flat leaf parsley
12 leaves	fresh mint

FOR THE DRESSING

1 clove	garlic, minced or micro-planed
⅓ cup	olive oil
2 tablespoons	lemon juice
1 teaspoon	dried oregano

Combine all the salad ingredients in a large bowl.

In a separate bowl, whisk together all the dressing ingredients. Pour the dressing over the salad and toss to coat.

Serve chilled.

Most Greek feta contains a combination of sheep and goat's milk. It is sheep's milk that gives feta its creamy tanginess while the goat's milk imparts a slightly drier texture. Today's Greek standards specify that feta cheese must be produced with at least 70 percent sheep's milk and a maximum of 30 percent goat's milk.

L.A. CHOPPED SALAD

makes 2-3 mains/4-6 sides

This is a bright and beautiful salad with all of the vibrant flavors of Latin America. It's a quick fix and a perfect addition to any picnic or barbeque as it goes best with sunshine and lively music.

Prep Time: 20 minutes + 8 hours soaking time for the beans
Cook Time: 15 minutes
Vegan, Gluten Free

FOR THE SALAD

½ cup	dried black or pinto beans (about 1⅓ cup cooked)
1	medium yellow bell pepper, medium chopped
½ cup	radish, thinly sliced
3 cups	tomatoes, seeded and medium chopped (about 6 medium variety tomatoes such as Roma)
2	ripe avocados, peeled, pitted and medium chopped

FOR THE DRESSING

1 clove	garlic, minced or micro-planed
2	green onions, white and some green parts, thinly sliced
¼ cup	lime juice
½ teaspoon	lime zest
2 tablespoons	honey
½ teaspoon	salt
¼ teaspoon	black pepper powder
¼ teaspoon	red chili powder
¼ cup	olive oil
¼ cup	fresh coriander, chopped

Rinse the beans and remove any stones. Cover the beans with 3 cups room temperature water and leave to soak for at least 8 hours.

Drain the beans and rinse them under running water. Place the beans in a pressure cooker along with 3 cups of water. Secure the lid on the cooker and place over high heat. Once the cooker builds enough pressure to release one whistle, reduce the heat to low and continue to cook the beans for 6 more minutes. After the 6 minutes are up, remove the cooker from the heat and allow the pressure to dissipate fully before opening. Drain the beans and allow them to cool.

In a large bowl, combine the beans, bell pepper, radish, tomato and avocado.

In a small bowl, whisk together all of the dressing ingredients. Pour the dressing over the salad and toss to coat.

Serve chilled or room temperature.

ROCCA SALAD

makes 3-4 sides

Rocca is a common find in many markets these days. In addition to arugula, it also goes by the names rocket, rucola, roquette, tira and Italian cress.

Rocca is one of the many names for the spicy arugula salad leaf. Though its names are many, its taste is unmistakable. A member of the mustard family, these leaves have a distinctive peppery flavor that really comes alive when combined with the tartness of sumac powder and fresh citrus. This is a chop, toss and serve salad than can be ready within minutes of finding those young pungent leaves.

Prep Time: 10 minutes
Cook Time: 0 minutes
Vegan, Gluten Free

FOR THE SALAD

3 ounces	rocca, washed, dried and trimmed (about 2½ cups loosely packed)
1	medium tomato, seeded and chopped small
2	green onions, white and green parts thinly sliced

FOR THE DRESSING

1 tablespoons	lemon juice
1 tablespoons	olive oil
¾ teaspoon	sumac
(⅛ teaspoon)	salt

With a sharp serrated knife, cut the rocca leaves into ½-inch strips. Place the strips in a large bowl along with the tomato and green onion.

In a small bowl, whisk together all the dressing ingredients. Pour the dressing over the salad and toss to coat. Salt to taste.

Serve chilled or room temperature.

BLANCHED VEGETABLE SALAD

makes 2-3 mains/4-6 sides

This is a hardy salad that always leaves me feeling satisfied, but not stuffed. A swift blanching not only enhances the color and texture of the vegetables, but also allows them to better absorb the dressing. The dressing is the same lively honey-lime dressing used in the L.A. Chopped Salad (p.57).

Prep Time: 20 minutes
Cook Time: 30 minutes
Vegan, Gluten Free

FOR THE SALAD

½ pound	potatoes, peeled and cut in ½-inch cubes (about 1 medium potato or cup prepared))
½ cup	green beans, trimmed and cut into 1-inch lengths
1 cup	baby corn, cut lengthwise then in ½
1½ cup	broccoli florets
1½ cup	cauliflower florets
1	small carrot, peeled and cut into ¼-inch thick discs

FOR THE DRESSING

1 clove	garlic, minced or micro-planed
2	green onions, white and some green parts, thinly sliced
¼ cup	lime juice
½ teaspoon	lime zest
2 tablespoons	honey
½ teaspoon	salt
¼ teaspoon	black pepper powder
¼ teaspoon	red chili powder
¼ cup	olive oil

Prepare a large bowl of ice water.

Place the potatoes in a large saucepan of lightly salted water over high heat. Bring to a boil then reduce the heat to medium and continue to cook until the potatoes are just tender throughout, about 5 minutes. With a slotted spoon remove the potatoes from the water. Submerge them in the ice water to stop them from cooking.

Replace the water in the pan with fresh lightly salted water and again, bring

to a boil. Working with 1 vegetable at a time, blanch the vegetables in the in the order in which they are listed in the ingredient list. Submerge the vegetable in the boiling water until its color brightens and it is just barley tender, about 20-30 seconds. Immediately remove the vegetable and submerge it into the ice water to stop it from cooking. Repeat until all the salad vegetables are blanched.

Drain all the vegetables and pat dry with a clean kitchen towel. Place the vegetables in a large bowl.

In a small bowl, whisk together all the dressing ingredients. Pour the dressing over the salad and toss to coat.

Serve chilled or room temperature.

CABBAGE SALAD/SLAW

makes 4-6 sides

One of the most universally available vegetables, cabbage in its many varieties plays a particularly abundant role in all of the seven continents. This cabbage salad offers clean flavors and a worldly flare that make it a versatile accompaniment. It's particularly nice served along side rich or fried foods.

Prep Time: 20 minutes + 1 hour sit time for the salad
Cook Time: 0 minutes
Vegan, Gluten Free

FOR THE SALAD

½ pound	cabbage, thinly sliced (about 3 cups loosely packed)
1	carrot, shredded
3	green onions, white and green parts, thinly sliced
⅓ cup	golden raisins
⅓ cup	walnuts, chopped

FOR THE DRESSING

2 tablespoons	white wine vinegar
2 tablespoons	lime juice
2 teaspoons	honey
½ teaspoon	dried oregano
¼ teaspoon	red chili powder
⅛ teaspoon	salt

Place the cabbage in a big pot or heat safe bowl and cover with boiling water. Allow the cabbage to sit uncovered in the water for 5 minutes then drain well.

In a large bowl, combine the cabbage, carrot, onion, raisins, nuts, vinegar, lime juice, honey, oregano, chili powder, and salt to taste. Toss to evenly distribute all the ingredients. Cover and refrigerate for 1 hour to allow the flavors to meld.

Serve chilled or room temperature.

NAAN SALAD

makes 4 mains

About a week before Christmas one year, my husband Brad and I headed to Chicago's twelve-floor Macy's department store (formerly Marshall Field's) on State Street eager to take in some of the holiday ambiance. After the necessary crowd battling, window gazing, line waiting and Frango mint purchasing, our blood sugar levels were wobbly at best. I vaguely remember the words Walnut Room, nice lunch, three-story Christmas tree coming from the direction of Brad's mouth as my eyes fell upon the line of people snaking out of the Walnut Room entrance, past the escalators, into, way into the world of pashmina shawl and handbag displays. Any images of potpie eating amidst Circassian Walnut paneling and Austrian chandeliers immediately vaporized as we did what any rational human would do, headed straight for the adjacent food court. Of course being Macy's it was quite a posh food court and I was incredibly pleased with a Mediterranean inspired salad that I got there. I've reproduced it many times since so I know it wasn't just the desperately low blood sugar making the judgment. Though I call it a salad, it's actually a generously topped open-faced sandwich best eaten with your hands than a fork.

Prep Time: 45 minutes + 10 hours soaking time for beans and 1½ hour standing time for naan dough

Cook Time: 20 minutes

FOR THE SALAD

8 cups	loosely packed salad greens
2	medium tomatoes, cut into ½-inch cubes
1	cucumber, cut into ½-inch cubes
1	onion, cut into thin strips
15	Kalamata olives, pitted
3 ounces	feta, cubed or crumbled

FOR THE VINAIGRETTE DRESSING

1 clove	garlic, minced or micro-planed
2 tablespoons	red wine vinegar
¼ cup	olive oil
¼ teaspoon	sugar
¼ teaspoon	salt
¼ teaspoon	black pepper powder

FOR THE ASSEMBLY

2½ cups	hummus (p.143)
4	naan (p.115 - ½ batch)

Prepare the hummus and naan.

In a small bowl, whisk together all the dressing ingredients.

In a large bowl, combine all the salad ingredients. Pour the dressing over the salad and toss to evenly coat. Adjust the seasoning if needed.

For each individual portion, cut one naan in half on the bias. Spread a generous amount of hummus on each half then top with ¼ of the salad.

Opposite page: Beans dry in the sun amongst views of the Himalayan Mountains of the Annapurna Trek, Nepal

MAIN
DISHES

MOMOS

makes about 30 momos

These Nepalese stuffed dumplings are steamed and served with a spicy tomato sauce. They were one of the first dishes our house man, Jeet, prepared for us when we lived in India. He would often fix them for us on nights we had Hindi lessons and did not get home until late in the evening. When we got home, we would delight in finding these little parcels neatly nestled in the steamer. A quick warm up and we'd tuck in! Jeet patiently showed me how to make these one evening and that memory has stuck with me. If only the Hindi had stuck the same.

Prep Time: 30 minutes
Cook Time: 30 minutes
Vegan

FOR THE SAUCE

2	medium tomatoes
1	green chili, trimmed and seeded
2 ounces	fresh coriander, leaves and stems (about 1½ cup loosely packed)
(½ teaspoon)	salt

FOR THE FILLING

1 tablespoon	oil
½ cup	baby corn, small chopped
⅓ cup	shelled peas
1 cup	cabbage, small chopped
½ cup	carrot, small chopped
2	small onions, finely chopped
1-2 cloves	garlic, minced or micro-planed
1 tablespoon	ginger, minced or micro-planed
(½ teaspoon)	salt
(¼ teaspoon)	black pepper powder
(2 teaspoons)	soy sauce
1 cup	fresh coriander, chopped

FOR THE WRAPPER

2 cups	all purpose flour
½ teaspoon	salt
1 teaspoon	oil
±¾ cup	water

Begin by preparing the sauce. Place the tomatoes in a small saucepan along with enough water to sufficiently cover them. Place the pan over high heat

and bring to a boil. Continue to boil the tomatoes for 10 minutes. Remove the tomatoes from the water and place them in a blender. Add the chili and coriander and blend until liquefied. Add salt to taste. Transfer the sauce to a small serving dish and set aside.

Heat the oil for the filling in a medium sized skillet over medium-high heat. Once the oil is hot, add all the vegetables except for the garlic, ginger and coriander. Cook the mixture for 3-4 minutes, stirring regularly. Add in the, garlic and ginger and cook for 2 more minutes. Season to taste with salt, pepper, and soy sauce. Stir in the coriander, remove the mixture from the heat and allow it to cool while you prepare the dough.

In a medium bowl, combine the flour, oil and salt. Use your hand to incorporate just enough water to form a tacky textured dough ball. Turn the dough out of the bowl onto a clean, lightly floured surface and knead until the dough becomes smooth and elastic, about 3-4 minutes.

To knead the dough, gather all the dough together into a pile. Using the heel of your hand, press firmly into the dough and slightly forward. Fold the far edge of the dough upwards, towards you, and press it down into the middle of the ball then away from you. Rotate the entire mass ¼ turn. Repeat this fold-press-turn sequence.

Roll the dough out approximately 1/16 inch thick. Then, using a round cookie cutter or rim of a glass, cut out circles approximately 3 inches (7.5 cm) in diameter. Gather the scraps and repeat as many times as necessary for the remainder of the dough.

To assemble the parcels, place about half a tablespoon of the filling in the center of a wrapper. Fold the wrapper in half around the filling so that the edges meet to make a semi-circle. Working your thumbs and fore fingers along the edges, seal the sides together with pleats. Repeat for the remainder of the filling.

Brush a perforated steamer pan lightly with oil to prevent the momos from sticking. Arrange the momos in the steamer basket with a bit of space in between to allow for some swelling. Place the steamer over a pot of boiling water making sure that the water does not touch the bottom of the steamer pan. Cover and steam for 10-12 minutes.

Transfer the momos to a serving platter, garnish with coriander leaves and serve hot or room temperature with sauce on the side.

INDIAN ENCHILADAS

makes 10-12 enchiladas

This dish is the story of Indian houseman meets Mexican cuisine. After working as a cook in the Mexican Embassy for a number of years, our houseman, Jeet, had developed a fondness for enchiladas, but some traditional Mexican ingredients can be expensive or difficult to find in India. Being a frugal and imaginative gent, he thought up this clever variation.

Prep Time: 25 minutes
Cook Time: 20 minutes

FOR THE SAUCE

1½ pound	tomatoes
	(about 9 of a medium variety such as Roma)
4	green chili, trimmed and seeded
1	extra large bunch fresh coriander, leaves and stems
	(about 5½ oz. or 4 cups loosely packed)
(1½ teaspoon)	salt

FOR THE FILLING

2 tablespoons	oil
1 cup	peas, shelled
4 cups	cabbage, thinly sliced (approximately 1 small head)
1 cup	corn kernels or baby corn cut into ¼'s lengthwise
1 cup	carrot, cut into 2-inch matchsticks
1 cup	green onions, green and white parts thinly sliced
(½ teaspoon)	salt
1-1½ cup	choice of melty cheese such as mozzarella, Chihuahua or queso fresco, shredded

FOR THE CHAPATTI WRAPPER

2 cups (10.4 oz.)	atta
1 teaspoon	salt
1 tablespoon	oil
±1 cup	water

FOR THE GARNISH

2 tablespoons	fresh coriander leaves

Preheat the oven to 350°F/176°C.

Begin by preparing the sauce. Place the tomatoes in a small saucepan of water over high heat. Bring to a boil. Continue to boil the tomatoes for 10 minutes. Remove the tomatoes from the water and place them in a blender.

Add the chilies and coriander and blend until liquefied. Add salt to taste then set the sauce aside for later.

Heat the oil for the filling in a large sized skillet or wok over medium-high heat. Once the oil is hot, add all the vegetables except the green onions. Cook the mixture until the vegetables are just becoming tender, about 3-5 minutes, stirring regularly. Stir in the green onions and half the coriander sauce and cook for 2 more minutes. Salt to taste. Remove the mixture from the heat and allow it to cool while you prepare the chapattis.

Prepare the chapattis as described on page 119.

Pour ½ cup of the sauce into a 9x13x3-inch baking dish. Spread the sauce to coat the bottom of the dish evenly.

Stir the grated cheese into the filling mixture, reserving a generous handful of cheese for the topping. Portion out ½ cup of the filling along the centerline of a chapatti. Roll the chapatti tightly and place it in the baking dish seam-side down. Fill, roll and place the remainder of the chapattis. Spoon the remainder of the sauce over the top of the enchiladas and sprinkle with the reserved cheese.

Bake until the filling is warmed through and the cheese is melted and nicely browned, about 20 minutes.

Garnish with coriander leaves and serve hot.

DAL FRY

serves 4

Dal fry was the first dish I ever prepared in a pressure cooker. I had eaten dal fry before as prepared by others and could attest to its comfort food quality of which most Indians speak, but discovering its speedy preparation in a pressure cooker was like coming across a genie in a bottle, nothing short of magic. Hot, flavorful, nourishing food would never be more than a couple of whistles away. This is my kind of fast food.

Prep Time: 20 minutes
Cook Time: 15 minutes
Vegan, Gluten Free

1½ cup	dried toor dal
½ teaspoon	turmeric powder
3	dried red chilies, stems removed
5	cloves
3 tablespoons	oil
1½ teaspoon	cumin seeds
⅛ teaspoon	asafoetida powder
1	medium onion, chopped
2	medium tomatoes, chopped
1 tablespoon	ginger, minced or micro-planed
2 cloves	garlic, minced or micro-planed
(2 teaspoons)	salt
(2 tablespoons)	lime, juiced and seeded (optional)
¾ cup	fresh coriander, chopped

Rinse the dal and remove any stones. Place the dal in the pressure cooker along with the turmeric, red chilies, cloves and 4 cups water. Secure the lid on the pressure cooker and place over high heat. Once the cooker builds enough pressure to release one whistle, reduce the heat to low and continue to cook the dal for 6 more minutes. Remove the cooker from the heat and allow the pressure to dissipate fully before opening.

Heat the oil in a small pot or skillet over medium heat. When the oil is hot add the cumin seeds and asafoetida. Cook until the cumin seeds begin to sputter. Add the onions and cook until tender, 4-5 minutes. Add the tomatoes, ginger, garlic, and salt and cook for another 3 minutes.

The addition of lime juice at the end not only adds liveliness to the final dish, but also helps increase the bioavailability of the iron present in the dal.

Stir the onion mixture into the cooked dal, Season to taste with salt and lime juice, if using. Stir in the coriander and transfer the dal fry to a serving dish.

Serve hot with rice or chapatti (p.119) on the side.

WARM MEDITERRANEAN
PEARL BARLEY

serves 4

This recipe was adapted from a food magazine out of the U.K. called Delicious. When my husband's parents came to visit us in Abu Dhabi from Chicago, we all enjoyed more than a couple leisurely dinners on the patio beneath our single palm tree. This salad was one of our favorites. It was perfect after a long day of sight seeing as it's quick to assemble. The warm, nutty taste of the barley is a comforting base for the creamy feta. With a nice heap of fresh greens stirred in, this salad always leaves me feeling satisfied and nourished.

Prep Time: 20 minutes
Cook Time: 20 minutes

FOR THE SALAD

1 cup	pearl barley
2 cups	cherry tomatoes, halved
½ cup	Kalamata olives, pitted and quartered
⅓ cup	pine nuts, toasted
3 cups	loosely packed bitter green, such as arugula
¼ cup	basil leaves, finely sliced
4 to 5 ounces	feta, crumbled

FOR THE DRESSING

2 tablespoons	white wine vinegar
2 tablespoons	lemon juice
1 clove	garlic, minced or micro-planed
⅓ cup	olive oil

To toast pine nuts, place them in a dry, thick-bottomed skillet over medium-low heat. Cook until the pine nuts become aromatic and lightly browned, about 3-4 minutes, shaking the skillet regularly to promote even toasting.

Rinse the barley and remove any stones. Place the barley in the pressure cooker along with 4 cups water. Secure the lid on the pressure cooker and place over high heat. Once the cooker builds enough pressure to release one whistle, reduce the heat to low and continue to cook for an additional 15 minutes. Remove the cooker from the heat and allow the pressure to dissipate fully before opening.

Meanwhile, combine the tomatoes, olives, nuts, bitter greens, basil and feta in a large bowl.

If using a hardier variety of bitter green, cut into thin strips.

In a small bowl whisk together the vinegar, lemon juice, garlic and olive oil. Pour the dressing over the salad mixture and toss to coat.

Drain the barley well and pour it, still warm, over the salad mixture. Cover the bowl with a tight fitting lid or cling wrap and allow to sit for about 15 minutes. This will help wilt the greens and melt the feta.

Stir the salad well then transfer to a serving dish and serve.

SPAGHETTI PUTTANESCA

serves 4

This authentically Naples style pasta translates literally as "whore's style spaghetti". Its racy name is linked with countless explanations for its conceptual origin in which prostitutes, bar owners, hungry customers or some combination there of tend to be reoccurring themes. Shameless by nature, this dish is salty, spicy, fragrant and cooked almost entirely from pantry ingredients. One can't help but appreciate it for being the real, unapologetic, in-your-face meal that it is.

Prep Time: 15 minutes
Cook Time: 20 minutes

¼ cup	olive oil
1	large onion, chopped
2 cloves	cloves, minced or micro-planed
½ teaspoon	chili flakes
3 cups	tomatoes, chopped
	(about 6 of a medium variety such as Roma)
⅓ cup	capers, rinsed
⅓ cup	Kalamata olives
¼ cup	flat leaf parsley, chopped, plus additional for garnish
8 ounces	dried spaghetti
(½ teaspoon)	salt
(¼ teaspoon)	black pepper powder

Bring a large pot of generously salted water to a boil.

Pour the oil into a large skillet over medium heat. When the oil is warm, add the onion and cook until soft, about 5 minutes. Add the garlic and chili flakes and cook for 30 seconds. Stir in the tomatoes and capers then reduce the heat to low and simmer until the sauce is thick and pulpy, about 10-15 minutes.

While the sauce is simmering, add the spaghetti to the boiling water and cook until al dente.

Stir the olives and parsley into the sauce.

Drain the cooked spaghetti and add it to the pan of sauce. Stir to coat the spaghetti evenly then season to taste with salt and pepper.

Transfer to a serving dish, garnish with parsley and serve hot.

PIZZA

serves 3-4

My husband and I are from Chicago. What can I say, we like pizza...a lot. We're a once a week kind of family. When we moved to the Middle East, there was some really great food to be had, but good pizza was simply not on our neighborhood's radar, and we missed our comfort food. So, what had once been an occasional weekend pizza experiment became a mission, a mission to develop a pizza recipe that would help fill that void. In the end, this is what we came up with. Thin, crispy crust with lots of slow cooked sauce as the base for whatever toppings we had on hand. I understand that toppings are personal, so I'll leave that up to you. We usually make 2 big pizzas, but you can just as easily make 4 individual pies from this recipe.

Prep Time: 20 minutes + 1-2 hours for sauce simmering and dough rising
Cook Time: 20 minutes

FOR THE DOUGH

1¼ teaspoon	dry yeast
2 teaspoons	sugar
2 tablespoons	corn starch
1½ cup	all-purpose flour, plus extra for kneading and rolling
1 cup	atta
¼ cup	corn flour/fine corn meal
1¼ teaspoon	salt

FOR THE SAUCE

1½ pound	tomatoes
	(about 9 medium variety tomatoes such as Roma)
10 cloves	garlic
1 tablespoon	dried oregano
1 tablespoon	dried basil
1 teaspoon	chili flakes (optional)
½ teaspoon	salt
½ teaspoon	sugar

FOR THE TOPPING

herbs/vegetables/cheese of your choice

FOR THE PREPARATION

cornmeal or semolina
(to prevent pizzas from baking to the pan)
olive oil

For the dough, measure out 1 cup of tepid water using a measuring pitcher. Add the yeast and sugar to the water, stir and set aside while you prepare the other ingredients.

Measure the corn starch, flours, and salt directly into a food processor then secure the lid. Once the yeast and sugar have dissolved into the water, turn the food processor on and pour the yeast solution through the top shoot in a slow, steady stream. It should take approximately 20 seconds for the dough to come together once all the water has been added. If the dough appears too dry, add a small amount of water. Likewise, if the dough appears too wet add a little more all-purpose flour. Once the dough begins pulling away from the sides of the food processor and appears to be rolling over itself, wait 10 more seconds then stop the motor. Turn the dough out onto a clean, lightly floured surface. Knead the dough a couple of times just to smooth the outer surface. Divide the dough into 2 equal portions. Shape each portion into a smooth round ball. Lightly coat each round with olive oil and cover with a clean kitchen towel. Allow the dough rise in a warm, draft-free place for 1-2 hours. It should at least double in size before rolling.

Alternatively, the dough can easily be mixed and kneaded by hand.

To make the sauce, place the tomatoes in a small saucepan of water over high heat. Bring to a boil. Continue to boil the tomatoes for 10 minutes. Remove the tomatoes from the water and place them in a blender. Add the dried herbs, chili flakes, salt and sugar. Blend until liquefied. Transfer the sauce to a medium size skillet (cast iron is best) over high heat. Bring the sauce to a boil then reduce the heat to low, cover and simmer until pizza sauce consistency is obtained, about 45 minutes, stirring every 15 minutes.

Cooking acidic foods like tomato sauce in a cast-iron skillet increases the iron content of the food by as much as 20 times.

When the dough appears ready, preheat the oven to 475°F/246°C, or your oven's highest possible setting. Prepare your topping ingredients.

Take one of the dough rounds and roll it into a rectangular shape roughly ⅜-inch thick using just enough additional flour to keep the dough from sticking to the rolling pin or work surface. Transfer the rectangle to a sheet pan generously sprinkled with corn meal or semolina. Do the same for the second dough round. Spread the sauce over each crust and add your toppings. Generously drizzle with olive oil. Allow the prepared pizzas to rest while the oven reaches full heat.

Bake until the crust looks crisp and nicely browned and toppings look cooked, about 15 minutes.

RAJMA
(KIDNEY BEAN CURRY)

serves 4

My friend Tara introduced me to this special North Indian dish of red kidney beans in thick gravy. It is flavorful, hearty, healthy and prepared in one pot.

Prep Time: 20 minutes + 6 hours soaking time for beans
Cook Time: 35 minutes
Vegan, Gluten Free

1½ cups	dried kidney beans (about 3½ cups cooked)
3 tablespoons	vegetable oil
1 teaspoon	cumin seeds
1	medium red onion, chopped
4	medium tomatoes, chopped
1 tablespoon	ginger, minced or micro-planed
2	green chilies, trimmed, seeded and minced
3 tablespoons	coriander powder
1 teaspoon	turmeric powder
½ teaspoon	red chili powder
1 teaspoon	black pepper powder
(1 tablespoon)	salt
¼ cup	fresh coriander, chopped

Rinse the kidney beans and remove any stones. Cover the beans with 6 cups water and leave to soak for at least 6 hours.

Drain the beans and rinse them under running water. Set them aside.

Pour the oil into the pot of a pressure cooker over a medium heat. When the oil is hot, add the cumin seeds and cook for 30 seconds. Add the onions and cook until tender, about 5 minutes. Stir in the tomato, ginger, and green chilies. Then add the coriander (powder), turmeric, chili, and black pepper followed by the beans and 3 cups of water. Stir. Secure the lid on to the pressure cooker and increase the heat to high. Once the pressure cooker builds enough pressure to release one whistle, lower the heat to low and cook 13 more minutes. Remove the cooker from the heat and allow the pressure to dissipate fully before opening.

Remove the lid and return the pressure cooker to low heat. Salt to taste. Simmer uncovered over low heat until the gravy reaches your desired thickness.

Transfer the Rajma to a serving dish, sprinkle with fresh coriander and serve hot with rice or chapatti (p.119).

PUNJABI CHOLE
(SPICED CHICKPEA CURRY)

serves 4

This is a staple dish from the north Indian state of Punjab. Its heady flavors serve as an edible illustration of the individuals that come from this Pakistan border state. Having borne the burden of nearly every invasion throughout the centuries, Punjabis tend to be a resilient, practical, intrepid and intensely patriotic people. This signature Punjabi dish is as easy to enjoy and impossible to forget as the people who created it.

Prep Time: 15 minutes + 8 hours soaking time for beans
Cook Time: 45 minutes
Vegan, Gluten Free

3	tea bags of black tea
1½ cup	dried garbanzo beans (about 3 cups cooked)
1 inch	ginger, peeled and cut into ⅛-inch discs
1	cinnamon stick
1	whole black cardamom pod
3	bay leaves
3 tablespoons	oil
1½ teaspoon	cumin seeds
⅛ teaspoon	asafoetida powder
5	whole cloves
1½ tablespoon	besan flour
1-2	green chili, trimmed, seeded and minced
5	medium tomatoes, puréed
4 teaspoons	coriander powder
¾ teaspoon	black pepper powder
¾ teaspoon	turmeric powder
¼ teaspoon	red chili powder
1½ teaspoon	salt
¾ teaspoon	black salt (optional)
¾ teaspoon	garam masala powder
1½ teaspoon	dried mango powder
4	whole green chilies, for garnish

If opting to use either one of the quick soak methods, include the tea bags in the first cooking of the beans. See p.189 for details.

Steep the tea bags in 6 cups of hot water for 5 minutes then discard the bags. Rinse the beans and remove any stones. Cover the beans with the tea and leave to soak for at least 8 hours.

Drain the beans and rinse them under running water. Place the beans in the pressure cooker along with the ginger, cinnamon stick, cardamom, bay leaves and 3 cups of water. Secure the lid on to the pressure cooker and place over high heat. Once the cooker builds enough pressure to release one whistle, reduce the heat to low and continue to cook the beans for 13 more minutes. Remove the cooker from the heat and allow the pressure to dissipate fully before opening.

Heat the oil in a large pot over medium heat. Once the oil is hot, carefully slide in the whole chilies. Fry the chilies until the skins are nicely blistered, about 30 seconds. Remove the chilies and set them aside for later.

Add the cumin seeds, asafetida and cloves to the hot oil. Once the cumin seeds begin to sputter, stir in the besan flour and cook for 15 seconds. Add the chopped green chili and tomato purée and cook until the oil begins to separate out from the mixture, about 2-3 minutes, stirring occasionally. Stir in the coriander, black pepper, turmeric and red chili powders and cook for 1 minute. Stir in the salt, black salt if using, and cooked bean mixture. Increase the heat to high, bring to a boil then reduce the heat to low and simmer uncovered until gravy reaches your desired thickness. Remove the cinnamon stick, cardamom pod and bay leaves. Stir in the garam masala and dried mango powder.

Try substituting black-eyed peas or another variety of bean. Refer to p.189 for cooking times.

Transfer the chole to a serving dish, top with fried whole chilies and serve hot with rice, bhature (p.113) or chapatti (p.119).

INDIAN MASALA OMELET

makes 1 omelet

When the British brought the omelet to India, Indians made it their own by adding a bit of spice. These days, one will find this east-west fusion fare to be a standard breakfast offering everywhere in India from a roadside dhabba to a four-star restaurant.

Prep Time: 5 minutes
Cook Time: 5 minutes
Gluten Free

1	egg
2 teaspoons	water
⅛ teaspoon	turmeric powder
¼ teaspoon	garam masala powder
1 tablespoon	oil or ghee
1 tablespoon	onion, chopped small
2 tablespoons	tomato, chopped small
1	green chili, trimmed, seeded and minced
10	fresh coriander leaves
generous pinch	salt
generous pinch	ground black pepper powder

Beat the egg, water, turmeric and garam masala together until just well mixed, not yet frothy. Mix in the onion, tomato, chili and coriander leaves.

A little water gives this omelet its thin delicate consistency.

Heat a medium size skillet over medium heat. Add the oil and gently swirl it in the pan to ensure the entire surface of the pan is coated. Pour the egg mixture into the pan. Slowly tilt the pan around in a circle and allow the mixture to spread thin all the way to the edges of the pan. Season the egg with salt and pepper.

For best results, choose a well-seasoned skillet with sloping sides.

Allow the first side to cook to a golden color, about 1-2 minutes. Flip the egg over and cook the second side. Do not over cook. Slide the omelet onto a plate.

Serve the omelet immediately with toast.

KITCHADI

makes 2 quarts

This Indian porridge is really a cross between a creamy rice cereal and a light lentil soup. I usually opt for the olive oil instead of the more traditional ghee, but either works well.

Prep Time: 15 minutes
Cook Time: 30 minutes
Vegan, Gluten Free

1 cup	basmati rice
½ cup	mung beans, sprouted
2 tablespoons	olive oil or ghee, plus additional for garnishing
½ teaspoon	cumin seeds
½ teaspoon	mustard seeds
1 teaspoon	coriander seeds
⅛ teaspoon	asafoetida powder
1 teaspoon	turmeric powder
1 teaspoon	coriander powder
1 teaspoon	cumin powder
1 tablespoon	ginger, minced or micro-planed
2 cups	mixed vegetables such as tomato, carrot, cauliflower, green beans, squash, potato, chopped small
(1½ teaspoon)	salt
½ cup	fresh coriander, chopped

Rinse the mung beans and rice and place them in a pressure cooker along with 6 cups of water. Secure the lid on the cooker and place it over high heat. Once the cooker builds enough pressure to release one whistle, reduce the heat to low and continue to cook for an additional 5 minutes. Remove the cooker from the heat and allow the pressure to dissipate fully before opening.

For instruction for sprouting your own mung beans refer to side note on p.21

Pour the oil or ghee into a medium size pot over medium heat. Once the oil is hot, add the cumin seeds, mustard seeds, coriander seeds and asafoetida and cook until the seeds begin to sputter. Add the turmeric, coriander (powder), cumin and ginger and cook for 20 seconds. Stir in the vegetables along with 1 cup of water. Continue to cook until the vegetables are cooked through, about 6-10 minutes, adding more water if needed to keep the mixture from catching.

Stir the spice-vegetable mixture and 1 cup of water into the cooked rice-bean mixture. Return to a boil then lower the heat to low, cover (with flat lid, not sealed pressure cooker lid) and simmer until desired consistency is reached. Season to taste with salt, remove from the heat and stir in the fresh coriander.

Portion the kitchadi into serving bowls and serve hot with a drizzle of olive oil or ghee on top.

SIMPLE KITCHADI

makes 2 quarts

At first glance, kitchadi may seem like a simple mixture of rice and mung beans, but to those in the know, it is delicious, nutritious food of the Gods. Simple kitchadi is quite appropriate when recovering from illness or anytime the body is calling out for a little special attention or healing tenderness. It is truly food that calms and comforts the body and psyche. Ayurvedic physicians often prescribe kitchadi to support healing on all levels. This variation is based on a recipe from Dr. Lad, a prominent ayurvedic doctor.

Prep Time: 15 minutes

Cook Time: 30 minutes

Vegan, Gluten Free

¾ cup	basmati rice
¾ cup	dried mung dal
2 tablespoon	olive oil or ghee, plus additional for garnishing
½ teaspoon	cumin seeds
¾ teaspoon	coriander seeds
⅛ teaspoon	asafetida powder
¼ teaspoon	turmeric powder
¼ teaspoon	coriander powder
1½ cup	mixed vegetables such as carrot, cauliflower, green beans, squash, chopped small (optional)
(1 teaspoon)	salt
¼ cup	fresh coriander, chopped

Kitchadi provides the body with both solid nutrition and ease of digestion. The combination of rice and mung dal equates to a complete protein (one in which all nine essential amino acids are present).
The simplicity of kitchadi can provide the body with a break from the work of constant processing required by more complex foods.

When eating kitchadi to support ayurvedic cleansing techniques such as Pancha Karma, do use ghee as it is best for stimulating the flow of fluids throughout the entire body and removing blockages.

Sort through the dal and remove any stones. Rinse the dal and rice then place them in a pressure cooker along with 6 cups of water. Secure the lid on the cooker and place it over high heat. Once the cooker builds enough pressure to release one whistle, reduce the heat to low and continue to cook for an additional 5. Remove the cooker from the heat and allow the pressure to dissipate fully before opening.

Pour the oil or ghee into a medium size pot over medium heat. Once the oil is hot, add the cumin seeds, coriander seeds and asafoetida and cook until the seeds begin to sputter. Add the turmeric and coriander (powder) and cook for 20 seconds. If including vegetables, stir them in along with ½ cup water. Continue to cook until the vegetables are cooked through, about 5 minutes, adding more water if needed to keep the mixture from catching.

Stir the spice-vegetable mixture and 1 cup of water into the cooked rice-dal mixture. Return to a boil then lower the heat to low, cover (with flat lid, not sealed pressure cooker lid) and simmer until desired consistency is reached.

Season to taste with salt, remove from the heat and stir in the fresh coriander.

Portion the kitchadi into serving bowls and serve hot with a drizzle of olive oil or ghee on top.

Opposite page: A vegetable vender displays her goods along a roadside in Kathmandu, Nepal

VEGETABLE DISHES

ALOO GHOBI (POTATO AND CAULIFLOWER)

serves 4

This is my absolute all time favorite 'subzi', or vegetable dish. I'm pretty sure that both cauliflower and potato were created with Indian spices in mind, each fissure of the floret and starch of the spud ready to be infiltrated with serious flavor. When I see the stark potato and cauliflower meet with those bright spices in the pan, I'm reassured that things are as they should be.

Prep Time: 20 minutes
Cook Time: 35 minutes
Vegan, Gluten Free

1½ teaspoon	salt
1 teaspoon	coriander powder
½ teaspoon	red chili powder
½ teaspoon	turmeric powder
2 tablespoons	oil
½ teaspoon	mustard seeds
¼ teaspoon	black peppercorns
1 teaspoon	coriander seeds
2	small onions, chopped
4 cloves	garlic, minced or micro-planed
1 tablespoon	fresh ginger, minced or micro-planed
1	medium tomato, puréed
1	bay leaf
1	medium head cauliflower, pared into florets
1 pound	potatoes, peeled and cut into 1-inch cubes (about 2 medium potatoes or 2 cups prepared)
2	small heads cauliflower, pared into florets
½ teaspoon	garam masala powder
1 tablespoon	fresh coriander, chopped

Combine the salt, red chili powder, coriander powder and turmeric powder with ½ cup of water and set aside.

Pour the oil into a large pan over medium heat. Once the oil is hot, add the mustard seeds, peppercorns, and coriander seeds. Cook until the mustard seeds begin to sputter, about 20 seconds. Add the onions and cook until they are transparent, approximately 5 minutes, stirring and scraping the bottom of the pan occasionally. Stir in the garlic, ginger, tomato purée and bay leaf and cook for 1 additional minute.

Stir in the potatoes along with 1 cup water. Cover and cook until the potatoes seem about half cooked through, about 10 minutes, stirring occasionally. Pour in the spice-water mixture followed by the cauliflower. Stir to coat all the vegetables evenly with the spice mixture. Cover and cook until both the potatoes and the cauliflower are tender, about 7-10 minutes, stirring occasionally.

Stir in garam masala powder and transfer to a serving dish. Top with fresh coriander and serve hot.

It is a good idea to keep a container of water within reach while preparing Indian potato dishes.
If, at any time during the cooking, the mixture begins to catch or stick to the pan, adding a small amount of water helps it release.

MATAR PANEER
(PEAS AND COTTAGE
CHEESE)

serves 4

Fresh peas always seem to embody the brilliance of spring. Those tiny green rounds popped straight from the pod rival the sweetness of candy. Perfection like this lends itself to simple dishes like this classic North Indian curry. Punjabis and Delhi-ites alike have long enjoyed this dish's combination of bright, earthy and creamy. So easy to prepare, it's safe to say that most Indians can whip it together with one hand while sipping a chai and perusing the latest Bollywood gossip magazine.

Prep Time: 15 minutes
Cook Time: 35 minutes
Gluten Free

3 tablespoons	oil
1 tablespoon	cumin seeds
2	small onions chopped
2 tablespoons	ginger, micro-planed
5 cloves	garlic, micro-planed
1½ pound	tomatoes, chopped
	(about 9 of a medium variety such as Roma)
½ teaspoon	red chili powder
1 tablespoon	coriander powder
½ teaspoon	turmeric powder
1½ cup	peas
(1 teaspoon)	salt
12 ounces	paneer, cut into 1-inch cubes
1½ teaspoon	garam masala powder
½ cup	coriander, chopped

Find a recipe for paneer on p.145

Pour the oil into a large skillet over medium heat. Once the oil is hot add the cumin seeds. When the seeds begin to sputter add the onions. Cook until the onions are tender and nicely browned, about 8-10 minutes. Add the ginger, and garlic and cook for 30 seconds. Add the tomatoes and cook till they break down into the mixture, about 8 minutes. Stir in the red chili, coriander (powder) and turmeric. Continue to cook till the oil begins to separate out of the mixture, about 5 minutes, stirring often. Once you notice the sheen of the oil, stir in the peas along with 2 cups water. Bring to a boil then reduce the heat and a simmer until the peas are cooked through and the gravy reaches

your desired consistency, about 5-10 minutes. Stir in the paneer and heat through. Salt to taste. Stir in the garam masala and coriander.

Transfer the matar paneer to a serving dish and serve hot with rice or chapatti (p.119).

DUM ALOO
(BABY POTATO CURRY)

serves 3

This dish steams baby potatoes in a thick yogurt and spice curry giving those humble little potatoes big tangy flavor. Any upstanding Kashmiri would argue it is a delicacy of main dish caliber and I agree whole-heartedly.

Prep Time: 30 minutes
Cook Time: 20 minutes
Vegan, Gluten Free

1 pound	baby potatoes, peeled
	(about 2 cups prepared)
1 tablespoon	sesame seeds, toasted or tahini paste
¼ cup	yogurt
1 tablespoon	ginger, minced or micro-planed
1 tablespoon	coriander powder
1 teaspoon	fennel seed powder
½ teaspoon	turmeric powder
½ teaspoon	red chili powder
½ teaspoon	paprika powder
2 tablespoons	oil
1 teaspoon	cumin seeds
⅛ teaspoon	asafoetida powder
1 tablespoon	besan flour
3	whole dried red chilies
1 teaspoon	salt
½ teaspoon	garam masala powder
¼ cup	fresh coriander, chopped

I usually use very small, bite size baby potatoes (about 1 to 1½ inch in diameter). Though somewhat tedious to peel, they make for a very nice presentation. If you use larger potatoes, cut them down into 1-inch pieces.

Place the potatoes in the pressure cooker and cover by 1 inch with generously salted water. Secure the lid on the cooker and place it over high heat. Once the cooker builds enough pressure to release one whistle, reduce the heat to low and continue to cook the potatoes for 1 additional minute. Remove the cooker from the heat and allow the pressure to dissipate fully before opening. Drain the potatoes and set them aside.

If using whole toasted sesame seeds, use a spice or coffee grinder to grind them into a fine powder. In a small bowl, combine the sesame powder or tahini paste together with the yogurt, ginger, and powdered coriander, fennel, turmeric, red chili, and paprika. Set aside.

Pour the oil into a medium size pot over medium heat. Once the oil is hot, add the cumin seeds and asafoetida. When the cumin seeds begin to sputter, stir in the besan flour and whole red chilies and cook for 20 seconds.

Stir in the yogurt-spice mixture and continue to stir. At first, the mixture will come together like a soft dough ball. After 2-3 minutes of stirring, the oils will begin to separate out. Once the mixture loosens and appears glossy, stir in the salt and ½ cup of water. Add the potatoes and stir to coat. Increase the heat to high and bring to a boil then reduce the heat, cover and simmer for 3 minutes, stirring occasionally. Remove the dum aloo from the heat and stir in the garam masala and fresh coriander.

Transfer the dum aloo to a serving dish, and serve hot.

PALAK PANEER (SPINACH AND COTTAGE CHEESE)

makes about 5 cups / serves 4

This creamy curry combines fresh spinach and Indian cottage cheese. It's nothing short of dreamy when scooped up by warm naan.

Prep Time: 15 minutes
Cook Time: 25 minutes
Gluten Free

1½ pound	spinach leaves, washed well
	(about a 3 pound bunch including stems)
4 ounces	fresh coriander, leaves and stems
	(about 3 cups loosely packed)
1 cup	yogurt
2 tablespoons	oil
1	small onion chopped
10 cloves	garlic, minced
3	green chilies, trimmed, seeded and chopped
1 tablespoon	coriander powder
1 teaspoon	cumin powder
½ teaspoon	turmeric powder
¼ teaspoon	black salt (optional)
8 ounces	paneer, cut into 1-inch cubes
1 tablespoon	lime juice
(¼ teaspoon)	salt

Find a recipe for paneer on p.145

Begin by blanching the spinach. Prepare a large bowl of ice water. Bring a large pot of lightly salted water to a rolling boil. Add the spinach to the water and cook just until its color turns a vibrant green, about 20 seconds. With a slotted spoon or tongs, remove the spinach from the water and immediately submerge it into the ice water. Allow the spinach to cool thoroughly in the ice water, about 2 minutes. Lightly drain the spinach then transfer it to the blender along with the coriander and yogurt. Blend the greens and yogurt into a smooth purée. This should render roughly 5 cups of purée. Leave this in the blender for later.

Pour the oil into a large skillet over medium heat. Once the oil is hot, add the onions and cook until tender and translucent, about 5 minutes. Add the garlic

and chilies and cook for 30 seconds. Stir in the powdered coriander, cumin, turmeric and black salt if using and cook another 30 seconds. Add the onion-spice mixture to the blender of green purée and blend until smooth. Transfer the purée mixture back to the skillet over medium heat, stir in the paneer, and gently bring to a boil. Salt to taste and stir in the lime juice.

Palak paneer served along side corn or pita chips makes for a delicious and healthy alternative to your standard spinach dip.

Transfer the palak paneer to a serving dish and serve hot with rice, naan (p.115) or chapatti (p.119).

ALOO MASALA
(SPICED POTATOES)

serves 4

This potato dish is essentially the filling for a masala dosa, the paper thin, crispy south Indian crepe made with fermented rice and dal batter. Although I determined long ago that I possess neither the patience nor skill to make a respectable dosa, I often make its delicious filling an easy potato side dish or even a quick lunch.

Prep Time: 15 minutes + 30 minutes soaking time for the dal
Cook Time: 25 minutes
Vegan, Gluten Free

1 tablespoon	toor dal
1 pound	potatoes, peeled and cut into 1-inch cubes or wedges (about 2 medium potatoes or 2 cups prepared)
2 tablespoons	oil
2 teaspoons	mustard seed
1 teaspoon	cumin seed
⅛ teaspoon	asafoetida powder
1 teaspoon	turmeric powder
1 tablespoon	ginger, minced or miro-planed
12	curry leaves
1	green chili, trimmed, seeded and minced
½ teaspoon	salt
1 teaspoon	lime juice
¼ cup	fresh coriander, chopped

Rinse the dal and remove any stones. Place the dal in a small, heat safe bowl. Cover the dal with 1 cup boiling water and allow to soak for at least 30 minutes then drain.

Place the potatoes in the pressure cooker and cover by 1 inch with generously salted water. Secure the lid on the cooker and place it over high heat. Once the cooker builds enough pressure to release one whistle, reduce the heat to low and continue to cook the potatoes for 1 additional minute. Remove the cooker from the heat and allow the pressure to dissipate fully before opening. Drain the potatoes and set them aside.

Pour the oil into a medium sized pot over medium heat. When the oil is hot, add the mustard seeds, cumin seeds and toor dal. Once the seeds begin to sputter, stir in the asafoetida followed by the turmeric, ginger, curry leaves and chili. Stir in the potatoes, salt and ¼ cup water. Cover and cook until the

potatoes are extra tender, about 2-3 minutes, stirring occasionally and adding additional water if the mixture begins to catch. Stir in the lime juice and coriander.

Transfer the aloo masala to a serving dish and serve hot.

SAUTÉED SESAME SPINACH

serves 4

This is a real quick preparation that can be applied not just to spinach, but to all kinds of vegetables for an easy Asian twist. It never ceases to amaze me how an enormous bundle of greens can cook down to such a fractional amount so make sure you grab a generous amount of your leafy vegetables.

Prep Time: 15 minutes
Cook Time: 10 minutes
Vegan, Gluten Free

1 pound	spinach leaves, washed well
	(about 12 cups loosely packed)
1 tablespoon	oil
1-2 cloves	garlic, minced or micro-planed
¼ teaspoon	black pepper powder
1 teaspoon	soy sauce
2 teaspoons	sesame seeds, toasted
(½ teaspoon)	salt

Begin by blanching the spinach. Prepare a large bowl of ice water and bring a large pot of lightly salted water to a rolling boil. Add the spinach to the water and cook just until its color turns a vibrant green, about 20 seconds. With a slotted spoon or tongs, remove the spinach from the water and immediately submerge it into the ice water. Allow the spinach to cool thoroughly in the ice water, about 2 minutes. Drain the spinach then place it in a clean kitchen towel. Gather the towel around the spinach, twist and squeeze to remove any excess water from the leaves. Coarsely chop the wrung spinach.

Pour the oil into a large skillet or wok over low heat. Once the oil is warmed, add the garlic and cook for 30 seconds. Add the spinach and raise the heat to medium. Add the soy sauce and pepper and cook until the spinach is warmed through, about 2-3 minutes. Sprinkle in the sesame seeds. Salt to taste then transfer to a serving dish. Drizzle with olive oil if desired.

Serve warm or room temperature.

To toast the sesame seeds, place them in a dry, thick-bottomed skillet over low heat. Cook until the seeds become aromatic and lightly browned, about 3-4 minutes, shaking the skillet regularly to promote even browning.

ALOO MATAR
(POTATO AND PEA)

serves 4

Another classic Punjabi vegetable dish, Aloo Matar utilizes two of the most versatile ingredients in nature, potatoes and peas. I like mine dry with the potatoes partly smashed so that the peas can happily nestle into the warm, curried embrace of the potatoes.

Prep Time: 10 minutes

Cook Time: 25 minutes

Vegan, Gluten Free

1 pound	potatoes, peeled and cut into 1-inch cubes or wedges (about 2 medium potatoes or 2 cups prepared)
1	green chili, trimmed, seeded and minced
1 teaspoon	ginger, minced or micro-planed
¼ teaspoon	red chili powder
¼ teaspoon	turmeric powder
2 tablespoons	coriander powder
2 tablespoons	oil
1 teaspoon	cumin seeds
⅛ teaspoon	asafoetida powder
¾ cup	peas
1 teaspoon	salt
½ teaspoon	garam masala powder
1	medium tomato, chopped small
2 tablespoons	fresh coriander, chopped

Place the potatoes in the pressure cooker and cover by 1 inch with generously salted water. Secure the lid on the cooker and place it over high heat. Once the cooker builds enough pressure to release one whistle, reduce the heat to low and continue to cook the potatoes for 1 additional minute. Remove the cooker from the heat and allow the pressure to dissipate fully before opening. Drain the potatoes and set them aside.

In a small bowl, combine the green chili, ginger, chili powder, turmeric powder and coriander powder with ¼ cup water and set aside.

Pour the oil into a medium sized pot over medium heat. Once the oil is hot, add the cumin seeds. When the seeds begin to sputter, add the asafoetida followed by the spice solution. Cook for 30 seconds then add the peas along

with ½ cup of water. Allow the mixture to cook 2 minutes then add the potatoes and salt. With the back of a large spoon, mash about a quarter of the potatoes. This will help create a thick gravy. Add ¾ cup of water and bring to a boil. Lower the heat and simmer until the gravy nicely coats the potatoes and peas.

Remove from the heat. Stir in the gram masala and tomatoes. Cover the pot for 5 minutes to allow the tomatoes to warm through.

Transfer the aloo matar to a serving dish. Top with fresh chopped coriander and serve hot.

Opposite page: Two local boys man the tandoor during a wedding in Rishikesh, India.

The Paisley Palate Cookbook   111

BREADS

BHATURE

makes 8-10 bhature

The first time I saw these voluptuous football shaped poofs was during my first ever experience at a Haldiram's Restaurant outside of Delhi. Near clueless to the what's what of Indian food, I spent a good ten minutes walking around the place asking perfect strangers with good looking trays, "Excuse me, what's that called?" There was a particularly long line for what I would come to know as Chole Bhature. Gorgeously spiced chickpea curry (p.87) accompanied by two of these freshly fried beauties. They are so beautiful, in fact, that I will occasionally put aside my annoyance with home frying to make these crispy yet chewy breads. Quite frankly, there is no tastier way to mop up a bowl of chole.

Prep Time: 30 minutes + 1-2 hours standing time for the dough
Cook Time: 20 minutes

±¾ cup	tepid water, divided
1½ teaspoon	dried yeast
1 teaspoon	sugar
2 cups (10 oz.)	all-purpose flour
¼ cup	semolina
½ teaspoon	salt
¼ cup	yogurt
	oil for frying
2 teaspoons	salt flakes

Place yeast and sugar in a bowl with ¼ cup tepid water, stir and set aside until dissolved, about 5 minutes.

Combine the flour, semolina, and salt in a large bowl. Make a well and pour in the yeast solution. Using your hand, begin working the mixture together. Continue to incorporate small increments of water until a tacky textured dough ball forms. Turn the dough out of the bowl onto a clean, lightly floured surface. Knead the dough until it becomes smooth and elastic, about 10 minutes, adding flour as needed to keep the dough from sticking to the work surface. Lightly coat the dough with oil, place it back in the bowl and cover with a clean kitchen towel. Let the dough rise in a warm, draft-free place for until it has doubled in size, about 1-1½ hours.

Turn the risen dough out of the bowl onto a clean, lightly floured surface. Knead the dough a couple of times then divide it into 8-10 equal portions. Shape each portion into a smooth round ball.

Heat the oil in a wok or wide pot over medium-high heat. The oil is ready when a small piece of the dough dropped into the oil immediately floats back to the surface. If you are using a candy/fry thermometer, this is 375°F/190°C.

Once the oil is ready, use a rolling pin to roll one portion into a flat oval approximately ⅛-inch thick. Carefully slide it into the oil. It should immediately begin to swell as the air on the inside begins to expand. Using a slotted spoon, gently push on the puffing bhatura to encourage the expanding air into all the space. Once the bottom side is just golden brown, about 30-45 seconds, flip the bhatura over and allow the second side to cook. Remove the bhatura from the oil and place on newspaper or kitchen paper to drain. Lightly sprinkle with salt flakes. Repeat the same frying method for the remainder of the portions.

When frying bhatura, as with all fried foods, it is essential that the oil achieve full cooking temperature before frying begins. Frying food in oil that is not hot enough will cause the food to absorb excess oil and make it soggy. Remember, a greasy bhatura is a poorly fried bhatura.

Serve the bhature immediately.

NAAN

makes 10 naan

This leavened bread is beautifully bubbly and delectably chewy. Of course authentic naan is baked a traditional tandoor, a cylindrical clay oven. The flattened bread dough is slapped onto the vertical wall where it sticks and bakes in temperatures nearing 900°F. Indian bread straight out of the tandoor is my number one reason for going out for Indian food. There really is no substitute for the traditional tandoor baking method. Nevertheless, there is a certain satisfaction that comes from making your own beautiful breads and these little lovelies are certainly worth their finishing brush of ghee.

Prep Time: 20 minutes + 1½ hour cumulative standing time for the dough
Cook Time: 15-45 minutes depending on your choice of baking surfaces

±¾ cup	tepid water, divided
1¼ teaspoon	dried yeast
1½ teaspoon	sugar
2½ cups (12½ oz.)	all-purpose flour
1½ teaspoon	salt
2½ tablespoons	oil
¼ cup	yogurt
1-2 tablespoons	choice of garnish, such as fresh chopped garlic, coarse salt, sesame seeds, onion seeds, mustard seeds, nigella seeds, cumin seeds, or fennel seeds
¼ cup	butter or ghee, melted (optional)

Modern naan recipes will sometimes substitute baking powder for yeast in the name of time. Though this method does sacrifice some of the flavor and texture finesses, it eliminates the dough's need to sit and rise before baking. You can bake your dough right after adding all the ingredients and it will rise in the oven. In a time pinch, add 1 teaspoon of baking powder in with the flour mixture and eliminate the yeast all together.

Place the yeast and sugar and in a bowl with ¼ cup tepid water, stir and set aside until dissolved, about 5 minutes.

Combine the flour and salt in a large bowl. Make a well and pour in the oil, yogurt and yeast solution. Using your hand, begin working the mixture together. Continue to incorporate small increments of water until a tacky textured dough ball forms. Turn the dough out of the bowl onto a clean, lightly floured surface. Knead the dough until it becomes smooth and elastic, about 10 minutes, adding flour as needed to keep the dough from sticking to the work surface. Lightly coat the dough with oil, place it back in the bowl and cover with a clean kitchen towel. Let the dough rise in a warm, draft-free place until it has doubled in size, about 1 hour.

Turn the dough out onto a clean, lightly floured surface and knead it about 10 times before dividing it into 10 equal portions. Shape each portion into a smooth round ball. Lightly coat each portion with oil, cover with a clean kitchen towel, and leave to rise for another 30 minutes.

Place a pizza stone, inverted cast iron skillet or heavy-duty baking sheet on the center rack of the oven. Preheat the oven to its highest possible setting and allow the baking surface to heat fully through. This may take the better part of 30 minutes. I set up the oven when the dough begins its second rise. Once the dough portions have completed their second rise, fire up the broiler of the oven as well.

Dense baking surfaces such as a pizza stone or iron skillet require more time to preheat, but the higher thermal mass more closely mimics tandoor cooking.

Using a rolling pin, roll one dough portion into a long, flat oval or tear drop shape approximately ¼-inch thick. If using a garnish, sprinkle a couple pinches over the top and lightly press it into the dough's surface. Repeat this with as many portions as will fit on your baking surface at one time. I can fit 4 naan cross-wise on a standard baking sheet, but only 1 piece at a time on the bottom of my iron skillet. Transfer the dough portions onto your hot baking surface.

Depending on the feel of your dough, you may wish to dampening the surface of the rolled dough portion with a little water help the dough cling to the baking surface long enough to retain its shape. This also helps any garnishes adhere.

Bake until cooked through and bubbly brown, 3-5 minutes. If using butter or ghee, brush it on the naan while it is still hot. Wrap the naan in a clean kitchen towel to keep it warm while you repeat the baking process with the remaining pieces.

Serve warm.

ZA'ATAR FLATBREAD

makes 10 flatbreads

These handsome breads, so popular with the Lebanese and Turks, can be used in so many ways. I generally like mine beneath a generous smear of hummus or mutable, but I'm perfectly content just layering on a few slices of fresh tomatoes and olive oil. Though they're not laborious, they're not born of speed either. They require the kind of patience most people can only find on a lazy Sunday afternoon, but with a little planning you can enjoy them any day of the week.

Prep Time: 30 minutes + 2 hours cumulative standing time for the dough
Cook Time: 30 minutes
Vegan

±1 ¼ cup	tepid water, divided
1 teaspoon	dried yeast
1 teaspoon	sugar
3 cups (15 oz.)	all-purpose flour
½ teaspoon	salt
¼ cup	olive oil, divided
4 tablespoons	za'atar
1 tablespoon	salt flakes

Place the yeast and sugar in a bowl with ¼ cup tepid water, stir and set aside until dissolved, about 5 minutes.

Combine the flour and salt in a large bowl. Make a well and pour in the yeast solution and 1 tablespoon of the olive oil. Using your hand, begin working the mixture together. Continue to incorporate small increments of water until a tacky textured dough ball forms Turn the dough out of the bowl onto a clean, lightly floured surface. Knead the dough until it becomes smooth and elastic, about 10 minutes. Lightly coat the dough with oil, place it back in the bowl and cover with a clean kitchen towel. Let the dough rise in a warm, draft-free place until it has doubled in size, about 1 hour.

Look for za'atar in the ethnic aisle of your grocery or any Middle Eastern market or, even better, make your own (recipe on p.133).

Turn the dough out onto a clean, lightly floured surface and knead it about 10 times before dividing it into 10 equal portions. Shape each portion into a smooth round ball. Lightly coat each portion with olive oil, cover with a clean kitchen towel, and leave to rise for another 30 minutes.

Using a rolling pin, roll each portion into a flat round disc approximately ¼-inch thick. Cover the discs with your kitchen towel and leave to rise for a final 20 minutes.

Preheat the oven to 425°F/218°C. Gently transfer the dough discs onto baking sheets. Dip your fingertips in the remaining oil and use them as a brush to coat the tops of the discs. Create a dimpled texture by gently pressing your fingertips into the surface. Sprinkle each portion with za'atar and salt flakes.

Bake until the edges are just golden, about 10-12 minutes.

Serve warm or room temperature.

CHAPATTI (FLATBREAD)

makes 10-12 chapattis

A tava is a traditional Indian griddle used to make flat breads. It is large, round and either flat or slightly concave in shape. Traditionally made of iron, they can be found in a variety of metals these days.

These griddle-cooked flat breads are a staple as well as comfort food in any north or west Indian kitchen. The high gluten content in the flour allows for them to be rolled out nice and thin. I make mine using my friend Tara's technique because that is how I first learned. She uses a gas stove and cooks them first on a tava, then directly over the burner. But you can also make excellent chapattis on an electric stove. I've included instructions both cooking methods.

Prep Time: 10 minutes
Cook Time: 15 minutes
Vegan

2 cups (10 oz.)	atta
1 teaspoon	salt
1 tablespoon	oil
± 1 cup	water

In a large bowl, combine the atta, salt and oil. Add about ½ cup water and use your hand to work the mixture together. Continue to incorporate small increments of water until a tacky textured dough ball forms. Turn the dough out of the bowl onto a clean, lightly floured surface and knead until the dough becomes smooth and elastic, about 5 minutes.

Roll the dough into a long tube approximately 1 inch in diameter. This will make it easier to portion. Break off a portion of dough slightly smaller than a golf ball. With floured hands, roll it in your palms to form a ball. Place the ball on your work surface and use a rolling pin to roll it into a flat round disc approximately ⅛ inch thick (this will be approximately 5-6 inches in diameter). Use additional flour when needed to keep the dough from sticking. Turning the disc ¼ turn after each passing of the rolling pin helps to keep a round shape. Repeat this process for the remainder of the dough.

Heat a tava or large skillet (preferably cast iron) over medium-high heat. Take your first chapatti and place it on your cooking surface.

If cooking on a gas stove:

Cook until the top side darkens slightly in color and small air bubbles can be seen beginning to form just underneath the surface of the dough, about 20 seconds. Flip the chapatti and cook the other side until you see more bubbles, another 20 seconds. Turn a second burner to high. Using your tongs, carefully pick up the chapatti by the edge and put it directly onto the burner. Cook until the chapatti balloons and develops brown spots, 5 to 10 seconds. Then flip the chapatti over and cook until the underside balloons and browns again, 5 to 10 more seconds.

In some regions, chapattis are also called phulkas, meaning 'to swell up', because the bread puffs up like a balloon as it cooks over an open flame. The rapid heating causes the water in the dough to turn to vapor, which gets temporarily trapped in the chapatti.

Wrap the chapatti in a clean kitchen towel to keep warm.

If cooking on an electric stove:

Cook until the top side darkens slightly in color and small air bubbles can be seen beginning to form just underneath the surface of the dough, about 20 seconds. Flip the chapatti and cook the other side until you see more bubbles, another 20 seconds. Using your hand covered in a kitchen towel, press along the edges of the round while spinning the chapatti on the cooking surface. Once the chapatti balloons and browns on that side, flip it and do the same on the other side.

Using a pair of flat tongs helps prevent the fragile chapattis from ripping as they are flipped.

Wrap the chapatti in a clean kitchen towel to keep warm.

Serve warm.

VEGETABLE PARATHAS (VEGETABLE FLATBREAD)

makes 10–12 parathas

Indian breads are perfect for scooping up those gorgeous curry dishes, but some of them can be meals in and of themselves. These vegetable parathas are made by folding and rolling the dough to create flaky layers after cooking. Served with fresh chutney, these are a stand-alone meal that requires no excuses.

Prep Time: 15 minutes
Cook Time: 25 minutes
Vegan

1 cup	vegetable(s), grated or chopped small
1 cup (5 oz.)	atta
1 cup (4 oz.)	besan flour
1 tablespoon	ginger, minced or micro-planed
½ teaspoon	cumin seeds
½ teaspoon	coriander powder
2 tablespoons	oil + more for cooking
1½	salt
± 1 cup	water

Some of my favorite additions include any combination of boiled potato or squash, carrot, spinach, fenugreek leaf (methi) or paneer.

In a large bowl, combine the vegetables, flours, ginger, cumin seeds, coriander, oil and salt. Add about ½ cup water and use your hand to work the mixture together. Continue to incorporate small increments of water until a tacky textured dough ball forms. Turn the dough out of the bowl onto a clean, lightly floured surface and knead until the dough becomes smooth and elastic, about 5 minutes.

Break off a piece of dough slightly larger than a golf ball. With floured hands, roll it in your palms to form a ball. Place the ball on your work surface and use a rolling pin to roll it into a flat round disc approximately ¼ inch thick. This will be approximately 5-6 inches in diameter. Use additional flour when needed to keep the dough from sticking. Turning the disc ¼ turn after each passing of the rolling pin helps to keep a round shape. Lightly brush the topside of the disc with oil, fold the disc in half to form a half circle, and roll it in order to bring the two layers together. Now, brush the topside of the half circle with oil, fold in half to form a quarter circle and roll it to bring the four layers together as an elongated triangle shape. Repeat this process for the remainder of the dough.

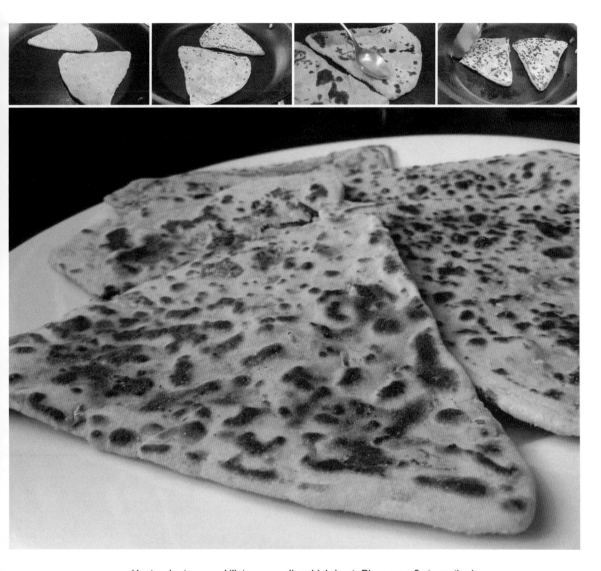

Heat a dry tava or skillet over medium-high heat. Place your first paratha in the pan and cook until you can see some discoloration of the dough showing through the topside, about 30 seconds. Flip the paratha over and cook on the second side for the same amount of time. Brush the first cooked side with a little oil then flip it over to cook it a second time until nice brown spots appear, about 30 seconds. Repeat this for the second side. In 3 flips of the paratha, you are dry cooking each side, then oil cooking each side.

Transfer the paratha to a clean kitchen towel and cover to keep warm.

Serve warm with choice of chutney (p.135-136) or harissa (p.141).

STUFFED PARATHAS (STUFFED FLATBREAD)

makes 8 parathas

When my husband and I first moved to India, we stayed at a company apartment for about a month while we searched for permanent accommodation. We soon discovered Dana Choga, the north Indian restaurant across the street, and made it an all too regular pit stop. They had a stuffed paratha with which I had a brief but ever so intense love affair. Once settled into our own place, I learned how to make stuffed paratha and eventually came up with a filling reminiscent to that of our Dana Choga days. Ah, love reunited sans the tandoor.

Prep Time: 20 minutes
Cook Time: 30 minutes
Vegan

FOR THE FILLING

8-12 ounces	potato, peeled, boiled and coarsely mashed (about 2-3 small potatoes or 1½ cup prepared)
2 tablespoons	oil
⅛ teaspoon	asafoetida powder
1 tablespoon	ginger, minced or micro-planed
10 cloves	garlic, minced
3	green chilies, trimmed, seeded and minced
1 teaspoon	cumin powder
2 teaspoons	coriander powder
½ cup	fresh coriander, chopped
2	green onions, green and white parts, thinly sliced
8 ounces	paneer, crumbled or chopped small
¼ teaspoon	salt

FOR THE DOUGH

2 cups (10 oz.)	atta
1 teaspoon	salt
1 tablespoon	oil
± 1 cup	water

I prefer a soft paneer for this filling. If you are making your own paneer as you can stop draining the whey once the soft, crumbly stage is reached. See Paneer recipe (p.145).

Pour the oil into a skillet over medium heat. Once the oil is hot add the asafetida, garlic, ginger and chilies and cook for 30 seconds. Add the cumin powder and coriander powder and cook for another 30 seconds. Stir in the potatoes, fresh coriander, green onions, paneer and salt. Remove the mixture from the heat and allow it to cool while you prepare the dough.

Prepare the dough exactly as you do for 1 batch of chapatti (p.119).

Divide the dough into 8 equal portions.

Roll one of the dough portions in your palm to form a ball. Place the ball on your work surface and use a rolling pin to roll it into a thick round disc approximately 3 inches in diameter. Shape the disc into a small bowl. Scoop 2 generous tablespoons of the filling into the center of the dough bowl then pinch edges together to seal the filling inside. Place the ball onto a well-floured work surface seam side down. Use a rolling pin to roll it into a flat round disc approximately ¼-inch thick. This will be approximately 5-6 inches in diameter. Use additional flour when needed to keep the dough from sticking. If the filling begins to show through the dough, gently rub some flour over the area and continue to roll. Flip regularly while rolling to ensure even distribution of the filling. Turning the disc ¼ turn after each pass of the rolling pin helps to keep a round shape. Repeat this process with the remaining dough and filling.

Heat a dry tava or skillet over medium-high heat. Place your first paratha in the pan and cook until you can see some discoloration of the dough showing through the topside, about 45 seconds to 1 minute. Flip the paratha over and cook on the second side for about the same time. Brush the first cooked side with a little oil then flip it over to cook it a second time until nice brown spots appear, about 30 seconds. Repeat this for the second side. In 3 flips of the paratha, you are dry cooking each side, then oil cooking each side.

Transfer the paratha to a clean kitchen towel and cover to keep warm.

Serve warm with chutney of choice (p.135-136) or harissa (p.141).

CORNBREAD

makes 9 pieces

Perhaps it's a result of a childhood spent under the big, bright stars of Texas, but I have a real soft spot for cornbread. So subjective and varied are regional preferences, that the exact degree of sweetness, density, graininess, and crumbliness of the perfect cornbread will most definitely be argued till the cows come home. I've tried countless recipes for "the best cornbread ever" and over time I've concocted a contender of my own.

Prep Time: 10 minutes
Cook Time: 30 minutes
Vegan

2 tablespoons	flax seed, finely ground
⅔ cup	choice of milk, such as soy, nut, rice, or cow
⅓ cup	oil
⅓ cup	honey
2-3	fresh green chilies, trimmed, seeded and minced (optional)
1½ cup (10½ oz.)	corn atta
⅔ cup (3⅓ oz.)	atta or flour of choice
1 tablespoon	baking powder
¼ teaspoon	salt

Flax seeds are available in brown and golden varieties and either will work equally well. Opt for the golden variety if you prefer the flax flecks to blend in amongst the golden hues of the corn.

In a large bowl, combine the flax seed with ¾ cup water and allow it to sit about 10 minutes.

Corn atta, or Makki Atta is fine, whole grain corn flour and can be found in most Asian food markets. Mexican corn masa flour could also be used and, depending on geographic location, may be more readily available.

Preheat the oven to 350°F/176°C. Lightly oil a 9x9x3-inch baking dish and set aside.

In a medium size bowl, combine the flours, baking powder, and salt.

Add the milk, oil, honey and chilies, if using, to the flax solution and whisk to thoroughly combine. Add in the flour mixture and use a rubber spatula to fold the ingredients together until the dry ingredients are just moistened. The batter will be little stiff. Pour the batter into the baking dish and spread evenly.

Bake until the edges turn copper brown and a toothpick inserted in the center comes out clean, about 20-25 minutes.

Allow the corn bread to cool for 10 minutes before cutting.

PAN CON TOMATE
(BREAD WITH TOMATO)

makes about 8 pieces

The first morning of a cycling trip through Costa Brava, I was intrigued by the basket of tomatoes and garlic cloves set, very intentionally, along side a loaf of bread on the breakfast buffet. Fast forward a couple of minutes of observation of the locals and I was enlightened and excited about my new favorite way to eat these modest ingredients. Pan con tomate is the brilliantly simple innovation of the Catalan Region in Spain. It is no more than toasted bread rubbed with garlic, topped with mushed perfectly ripe tomato, drizzled with olive oil and sprinkled with a bit of salt, but the combination magically comes together as more than the sum of its parts.

Prep Time: 5 minutes
Cook Time: 5 minutes
Vegan

1 pound loaf	rustic style bread, cut into ¾-inch thick slices
5 cloves	garlic, cut in half crosswise
4-5	medium tomatoes, cut in half crosswise
1 cruet	olive oil
small bowl	salt flakes

Lightly toast the bread slices on a barbeque or under an oven grill, 1-2 minutes per side. Plate the toasted bread along with the halves of garlic and tomato. Serve this with olive oil and salt on the side. Prepare while you eat.

To prepare, rub the cut side of a garlic clove over the toasted bread. Rub the cut side of a tomato over the bread, pressing firmly to push the pulp into the bread. Drizzle the bread with olive oil and sprinkle with a pinch of salt.

Opposite page: A woman and her daughter sell spices along the bank of the Godavari River in Nashik, India.

SPICES, SAUCES,
CHUTNEYS,
SPREADS, DIPS &
CHEESE

ZA'ATAR

makes about 1¼ cup

Za'atar is a traditional Middle Eastern and North African seasoning mixture made predominantly of thyme. The name za'atar is the name of both the wild thyme (Origanum syriacum) that grows all over the mountains and hills of the Middle East as well as the name of the mixture. Its taste is a synthesis of tangy, herbal, nutty, and toasty. In addition to flavoring or garnishing dishes, it can be mixed with olive oil and used as a marinade, dressing or bread dip.

Prep Time: 10 minutes
Cook Time: 0 minutes
Vegan, Gluten Free

¾ cup	dried thyme
¼ cup	sumac powder
¼ cup	sesame seeds, toasted
2 teaspoons	salt

Place the thyme, in a coffee grinder and grind into a fine powder. Mix together the thyme the sumac, sesame seeds and salt. Store in an airtight container.

Za'atar recipes vary from region to region and country to country. Though all preparations will include thyme, sumac, sesame seeds, and salt, other preparations may also include cumin, coriander, oregano, fennel, anise and/or cinnamon.

BASIC RED CHILI SAUCE

makes about 2 cups

Wander in a westward direction on Khari Baoli Road in Delhi's Chandi Chowk district and you'll soon find yourself in Asia's largest wholesale spice market. It is here that, supposedly, every spice on the planet is said to be available. The fragrances that spill out from the impossibly narrow and seemingly endless shops are nothing short of an assault on your nostrils and throat. Spice vendors sit comfortable and dry eyed amid the abrasive air, proudly interpreting the coughing, sneezing and eye watering of the passers by as a testament to the freshness of their spices. I am transported to Old Delhi every time we make this potent chili sauce. Its preparation has the potential to send anyone within a 20-foot radius into a coughing fit sure to swell any chili vendor's chest with pride.

Prep Time: 5 minutes + 30 minutes soaking time for the chilies
Cook Time: 0 minutes
Vegan, Gluten Free

3 ounces	dried red chilies, stems removed
	(about 2½ cups loosely packed)
1 teaspoon	salt
± 1½ cup	white vinegar

Place the chilies in a heat safe bowl, cover them with boiling water, cover the bowl and allow the chilies to soak 30 minutes. Drain well.

Place the chilies in the blender along with the salt and 1 cup of the vinegar. Blend on high till the mixture begins to come together and smooth out. With the blender still running, add the remaining vinegar through the feed tube in a thin stream until the mixture reaches your desired thickness. I like mine the consistency of a freshly melted milkshake, that is to say thick, but pourable with enough body to coat whatever it is I'm using it on.

Recycled condiment bottles make for pretty gifting and easy dispensing. This sauce will keep for 2 months, no need for refrigeration

MUMBAI HARI CHUTNEY (GREEN CHUTNEY)

makes about ¾ cup

Mumbai's famous vegetable sandwich is a three-tiered sandwich, each white sandwich bread slice buttered and chutney-ed. Layered inside are slices of boiled beetroot, boiled potato, onion, cucumber and tomato sprinkled with chaat masala. Crusts removed and cut into 6 triangle pieces is how a real Mumbian enjoys it.

The almonds are added to help preserve the vibrant green color which is nice if you don't plan to use the chutney right away.

An integral part of Mumbai's famous vegetable sandwich, this chutney is bright and tangy with a relatively subtle spicy bite. It can be put on anything for which you're craving that extra layer of flavor. It's sometimes called chaat, or snack chutney because it goes so well with any of the fried snack foods so popular on the streets of India.

Prep Time: 15 minutes
Cook Time: 0 minutes
Vegan, Gluten Free

2 tablespoons	lime juice
3-4	green chilies, trimmed and seeded
3	almonds (optional)
1 tablespoon	ginger, minced or micro-planed
⅛ teaspoon	asafoetida powder
¼ teaspoon	sugar
1 teaspoon	salt
±3 tablespoons	water
2 ounces	fresh coriander, leaves and stems (about 1½ cup loosely packed)

Place all the ingredients, except the water and coriander, in a blender and blend until smooth. Add the coriander and again blend until smooth, adding just enough water to bring the mixture together.

USEFUL COMBINATIONS AND RATIOS

Creamy Hari Chutney = 1 hari chutney : 1 yogurt

Hari Dressing = 1 hari chutney : 1 vinegar : 2 oil

LAAL CHUTNEY
(RED CHUTNEY)

makes about 1¼ cup

This little chutney is nice along side bean or lentil dishes such as Thukpa (p.29) or Rajma (p.85). It has a firm kick and some serious endurance that's sure to keep you feeling toasty even in the dead of winter.

Prep Time: 15 minutes
Cook Time: 0 minutes
Vegan, Gluten Free

1 pound	tomatoes
	(about 6 medium of a variety such as Roma)
3-4	dried red chilies, stems removed
1 clove	garlic
(½ teaspoon)	salt

Place the chilies in a heat safe bowl, cover them with boiling water, cover the bowl and allow the chilies to soak 30 minutes. Drain well.

Place the tomatoes in a small saucepan along with enough water to sufficiently cover them. Place the pan over high heat and bring to a boil. Continue to boil the tomatoes for 10 minutes.

Remove the tomatoes from the water and place them in a blender along with the chilies and garlic. Blend until liquefied. Add salt to taste.

Transfer the sauce to a small serving dish.

ROMESCO SAUCE

makes about 2 cups

This spicy, smoky, slightly sweet sauce from the Catalonia region in Spain is both handsome and versatile. It's a creamy roasted red pepper pesto that flatters appetizers, mains and sides alike. After trying it the way our friend Myra prepares it, using cashews instead of the traditional almonds, I've never made it any other way. The Catalonians serve it along side barbequed calçots, a variety of mild green onion native to that region. In keeping with this theme, a big bunch of fat green onions make for good dipping.

Prep Time: 30 minutes
Cook Time: 25 minutes
Vegan, Gluten Free

¼ cup	olive oil, plus additional for roasting
1 bulb	garlic
2	medium tomatoes, cut in half and seeded
4	medium red bell peppers, quartered and seeded
2	mild chili pepper, such as ancho, Anaheim or guajillo, cut in half and seeded
½ cup	cashews
1 tablespoon	red wine vinegar
½ teaspoon	paprika
¼ teaspoon	red chili powder (optional)
(½ teaspoon)	salt
(¼ teaspoon)	black pepper powder

FOR GREEN ONIONS

2 pounds	green onions, trimmed, bulbs slit in half
	salt
	black pepper powder

Prepare a barbecue or heat an oven grill to medium-high heat.

Trim the tip of the garlic bulb ½-inch to just expose the tops of the garlic cloves themselves then place the garlic on a sheet of aluminum foil. Drizzle the garlic with olive oil and seal the foil into a loose pouch around the bulb. Likewise, drizzle the tomato and chili halves with olive oil and seal them in their own foil pouch.

Place both foil pouches and the red bell peppers, skin side down, directly on the barbeque grill. If you are using your oven grill, place the pouches and peppers on a baking sheet, peppers skin side up toward the flame. Grill until

the bell pepper skins are nicely blistered and charred, about 20-25 minutes. Remove the bell peppers and foil pouches from the grill. Immediately transfer the bell peppers to a bowl, cover with a tight fitting lid or cling wrap and allow to steam for about 15 minutes. The steam will loosen the skins making them easy to peel off. Carefully open the foil pouches and allow the contents to cool.

Blend the cashews in a food processor until finely ground. Squeeze the garlic cloves out of their paper into the processor. Scrape the flesh from both the tomato and chili and add them as well, discarding the skins. Peel and discard the skin of the bell peppers and add the flesh to the processor. Add the olive oil, vinegar, paprika and chili powder, if using. Process until smooth adding a little water if necessary to create a soft dipping consistency, season with salt and pepper and transfer to a serving bowl.

Lay the green onions on a sheet of foil and season with salt and pepper. Seal the foil into a loose pouch around the onions and place directly on the barbeque grill or on a sheet pan under the oven grill. Grill the onions until softened and just charred, about 10 minutes.

Serve the onions warm along side the Romesco sauce.

BASIL PESTO

makes 3 cups

When basil comes into season you can quickly have more than you know what to do with. Basil harvest always means a significant batch of pesto, or two. Our family friend Peggy used to store her pesto in individual, ready-to-use portions by first freezing it in ice cube trays and later transferring the cubes to sealed storage containers, a small amount of work that equates to intense basil flavor available even after the growing season has passed.

Prep Time: 10 minutes
Cook Time: 0 minutes
Gluten Free

⅓ cup	pine nuts, toasted (optional)
3 cloves	garlic
12 ounces	fresh basil leaves, (about 3 cups packed)
½ cup	Parmesan, grated
¼ teaspoon	salt
¼ teaspoon	black pepper powder
½ cup	olive oil

Place the garlic and nuts, if using, in the food processor and process until finely minced, about 20 seconds. Add the basil, Parmesan, salt and pepper and process. With the processor running, pour the olive oil through the feed tube in a thin stream. Continue to process until the pesto becomes a loose purée, stopping the processor as needed to scrape down the sides of the bowl.

Transfer the pesto to storage containers and cover with a thin layer of olive oil before sealing. This will help prevent the outer layer from oxidizing and losing its vibrant green color.

Pesto will keep about a week in the fridge and up to 2 months in the freezer.

GUACAMOLE

makes about 2 cups

In my Chicago neighborhood of Logan Square, the large Latino population means that the corner store can always be relied upon to have all the fixings for great guacamole. In no time at all I can be scooping up this cool green dip with El Milagro Tortillaria corn chips delivered fresh that morning. There's no place like home.

Prep Time: 10 minutes
Cook Time: 0 minutes
Vegan, Gluten Free

2	ripe avocados
1	medium onion, finely chopped
2	medium tomatoes, finely chopped
1 cup	fresh coriander, finely chopped
¼ cup	lime juice
¼ teaspoon	chili powder (optional)
(1 teaspoons)	salt

Slice the avocados open and remove the pits. Scoop the pulp into a bowl and mash well with the back of a fork. Add the onion, tomatoes, cilantro, lime juice and chili powder, if using. Combine well then salt to taste.

Serve room temperature with corn chips.

HARISSA

makes 1½ cups

Two hundred grams of harissa, this was my standard grab from the deli counter in the Middle East. This is a seriously spicy chili paste that's commonly served as an accompaniment for many North African dishes. It is quick to whip up and can be used to boost the flavor of marinades, dressings, soups, vegetables and pasta sauces. My favorite is thinly smeared on toast or flatbread and topped with hummus. I use my dedicated coffee grinder for the spices and the food processor for the rest so the preparation takes no time at all. This batch is plenty large for you share with a chili-loving friend.

Prep Time: 30 minutes + 30 minutes soaking time for the chilies
Cook Time: 0 minutes
Vegan, Gluten Free

2½ ounces	dried red chilies, stems removed
	(about 2 cups loosely packed)
6 cloves	garlic
2 teaspoons	dried mint
2 teaspoons	coriander powder
2 teaspoons	cumin powder
2 teaspoons	caraway powder
1 teaspoon	salt
⅓ cup	olive oil, divided

Place the chilies in a heat safe bowl. Cover the chilies with boiling water and allow to them to soak for 30 minutes then drain well.

Place the garlic in the food processor and process until finely minced. Add the chilies, spices, salt and half the oil. Process for 20 seconds then scrape down the sides of the bowl. Add the remaining oil then process again. Continue to alternate processing and scraping down the sides of the bowl until a thick paste forms.

Transfer the harissa to a clean storage container. Cover with a thin layer of olive oil and seal. Remember to label and date your container.

Harissa will keep up to two months in the fridge. Make sure your storage container is extremely clean and dry prior to filling. Replace the thin top layer of olive oil as needed.

BABAGANOUSH

makes 2 cups

This creamy Middle-Eastern eggplant dip is always right beside the hummus in any traditional Middle Eastern meze. It has a smoky, roasted eggplant and tahini flavor that is nothing short of addictive.

Prep Time: 10 minutes
Cook Time: 30-50 minutes
Vegan, Gluten Free

2 pounds	eggplant
2 cloves	garlic
2 tablespoons	olive oil, plus additional for serving
¼ cup	tahini paste
2 teaspoons	lemon juice
(¾ teaspoon)	salt
(¼ teaspoon)	black pepper powder

Prepare a barbecue or heat an oven grill to medium-high heat.

Using a fork, generously prick holes in the eggplants. Place the eggplants directly on the barbeque grill or on a baking sheet under the oven grill. Grill them until they are scorched on the outside and soft throughout, about 30-50 minutes depending on their size. Rotate 2-3 times during this time. Transfer the eggplant to a bowl, cover with a tight fitting lid or cling wrap and allow to steam for about 15 minutes. Trim the end of each eggplant and peel away the skin. The skin should come off rather easily.

Place the garlic in the food processor and process until finely minced. Add the eggplant flesh, olive oil, tahini paste and lemon juice and process until light and creamy. Season to taste with salt and pepper.

Transfer the babganoush to a serving dish. Drizzle with olive oil and serve warm or room temperature.

For best results, look for firm, smooth-skinned eggplants that seem heavy for their size. Choose the "male" fruits, which have a round dimple at the blossom end, rather than the "female" fruits, which have an oval dimple. The over-mature females tend to impart bitterness due to an abundance of seeds.

Male (L) and female (R)

HUMMUS

makes about 2½ cups

The Arabic word hummus translates literally as chickpeas. It is believed to have originated from the Shami region (Lebanon/Jordan/Palestine/Syria), but disputes continue as to exactly who can claim it as their own. While the region bickers, the entire western world has fallen for this Middle Eastern dip. I like to make extra so I can quickly toss together Naan Salad (p.65) later on.

Prep Time: 10 minutes + 8 hours soaking time for beans
Cook Time: 15 minutes
Vegan, Gluten Free

1 cup	dried garbanzo beans (about 2 cups cooked)
4 cloves	garlic
⅓ cup	olive oil, plus additional for serving
4 teaspoons	cumin powder
⅓ cup	tahini paste
2 tablespoons	lemon juice
(1 teaspoon)	salt
± ½ cup	water (reserved from cooking the beans)
sprinkle	paprika powder, for garnish

The skins of the cooked garbanzo beans do not break down easily once they have cooled, so process the garbanzo beans while the beans are still warm in order to make a smooth hummus.

Rinse the beans and remove any stones. Cover the beans with 6 cups room temperature water and allow them to soak for at least 8 hours.

Drain and rinse them under running water. Place the beans in a pressure cooker along with 5 cups of water. Secure the lid on the pressure cooker and place over high heat. Once the cooker builds up enough pressure to release one whistle, reduce the heat to low and continue to cook the beans for 13 more minutes. Remove the cooker from the heat and allow the pressure to dissipate fully before removing the lid. Drain the beans, reserving about 1 cup of the cooking water.

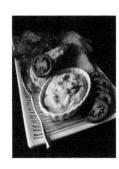

Place the garlic in the food processor and process until finely minced. Add the beans, olive oil, cumin, tahini paste and lemon juice and process until smooth. If the mixture is too thick add some of the reserved cooking water 1 tablespoon at a time until a creamy consistency is achieved. Season to taste with salt.

Transfer the hummus to a serving dish. Garnish with a drizzle of olive oil and sprinkle of paprika. Serve warm or room temperature.

Experiment with different varieties of beans, spices and herbs. Try rosemary-bean spread made by substituting cannellini beans for garbanzo beans and rosemary for cumin.

PANEER

makes about 1 cup

Paneer is a soft fresh Indian cottage cheese made using a simple acid and no rennet. From sweets, to snacks, curries and even flat breads, one or another form of this cheese is used extensively in North Indian cuisine. Paneer can also be used in vegetarian kebab and tikka preparations.

Prep Time: 5 minutes + 45 minutes draining time for firm texture
Cook Time: 20 minutes
Gluten Free

6 cups	whole cow's milk
3 tablespoons	lime juice + 1 additional tablespoon in reserve
½ cup	water

Combine the 3 tablespoons of lime juice and water and set aside.

Pots made of reactive metals such as aluminum and copper will react with the acid of the lime juice and impart a metallic taste to your paneer. A heavy bottom, non-reactive pot will prevent the milk from scorching while preserving the paneer's clean, creamy taste.

Pour the milk into a deep, heavy bottomed, non-reactive pot over medium-high heat. Stir occasionally as the milk heats. Just as the milk comes to a gentle boil, turn the heat down to low and stir in the lime juice solution a little at a time. The solid milk curds will begin to separate out and float to the top of the liquid whey. Continue to stir. You may not need to add all the lime solution, stop once the whey appears clear-green in color. If you add the entire quantity of your lime solution and the whey still does not appear clear-green, add the additional tablespoon of undiluted lime juice. Once the clear-green color whey appears, turn off the heat.

The nutrient and protein rich whey can be reserved and used in place of water or milk when making breads, smoothies or lassis.

Pour the separated milk through a strainer lined with muslin or cheesecloth. Rinse the milk solids under running water. This will cool the curds and wash away the lime flavor. Gather the cloth around the curds, twist and squeeze to remove the majority of the water. At this stage the paneer will be soft and crumbly, but hold its shape so you can roll a small piece into a ball. This soft paneer is ready to use. It is perfect in dishes such as paneer stuffed paratha (p.123) or in any recipes calling for farmer's cheese.

Soft paneer is also commonly used as a substitute for or in combinations with ricotta cheese in baked dishes like lasagna, ravioli or blintzes.

For a firmer paneer, one that can be cut into cubes and used in dishes like palak paneer, continue to drain the whey. Place the tightly cloth-bound curds on a clean work surface and place a heavy weight atop for an additional 30-45 minutes. For this, you can use a cast iron pan, a foil wrapped brick, a pot filled with dry beans, be creative.

Unwrap the paneer and cut as needed.

Cover any unused pieces with water and store in a sealed container in the fridge for up to 1 week.

1) Milk just before it begins to boil 2) Slowly adding the lime juice solution
3) Whey appears clear-green in color as the curds separate out 4) Straining the
separated milk 5) Drained curds 6) Soft paneer 7) Firm paneer

Opposite page: A happy Buddha statue of the Ubud Monkey Forest, a nature reserve and temple complex in Ubud, Bali.

SWEETS

OATMEAL DATE BARS

makes 9 bars

Soon after my husband and I moved to the Middle East, I began to research date bar recipes. I had never eaten a date bar in my life, but I just knew I would love them. For three years I had the most beautiful, delicious dates continuously available to experiment with and once I established this recipe, date bars and I quickly began making up for lost time.

Prep Time: 10 minutes
Cook Time: 25 minutes

FOR THE FILLING

1 cup	dates, pitted and chopped
½ cup	water
1½ tablespoons	sugar

FOR THE CRUST/CRUMBLE

1½ cup (4½ oz.)	quick cooking oats
1 cup (5 oz.)	atta or flour of choice
½ cup (4 oz.)	brown sugar
½ teaspoon	baking soda
¼ teaspoon	salt
¼ cup (2 oz.)	butter, melted or oil
1	egg white

If you only keep whole rolled oats on hand, give them a quick blitz in a food processor before mixing your dry ingredients together.

Preheat the oven to 350°F/176°C.

Lightly oil a 9x9x3-inch baking dish and set it aside.

In small saucepan over medium heat, combine the dates, water and sugar. Cook and stir until the mixture comes to a boil. Reduce the heat to medium-low and continuously stir until mixture is thickened, about 5 minutes. Remove the mixture from the heat and allow it to cool slightly.

In a large bowl, combine the oats, flour, brown sugar, baking soda, and salt. Pour in the butter or oil and egg white. Work the mixture with your hand until it is evenly blended with a crumbly consistency.

Pat half the oat mixture into the bottom of the baking dish. Spread the date mixture evenly over oat mixture. Then, sprinkle the remaining oat mixture on top.

Bake for 20-25 minutes or until lightly browned. Cool slightly and cut into bars.

TORTE DE LA ALMENDRA (ALMOND TORTE)

makes 1 torte

A traditional dessert from the Galician Region of Spain, this almond torte seems to be a dessert created for the purpose of loitering after a rambling Sunday meal reminiscing about travels in Northern Spain and the remarkable food the Spanish have to offer.

Prep Time: 20 minutes
Cook Time: 1 hour 20 minutes

3 cups (14 oz.)	blanched almonds, lightly toasted and finely ground
1 cup (5 oz.)	atta or flour of choice
2 teaspoons	orange zest
1¾ cup (12¾ oz.)	sugar
⅔ cup (5 oz.)	butter, softened
6	eggs
2 tablespoons	orange juice
2 tablespoons	powdered sugar, for garnish

Preheat the oven to 325°F/163°C.

Lightly grease a 9-inch spring form cake pan.

In a medium bowl, combine the ground almonds, flour and orange zest and set aside.

In the bowl of an electric stand mixer, cream together the butter and sugar until it is light and fluffy, about 3 minutes on medium speed. Add the eggs one at a time, beating well after each addition. Remove the bowl from the mixer and use a rubber spatula to fold in the flour mixture until the ingredients are just combined. The batter should be slightly lumpy. Do not over mix. Pour the batter into the cake pan.

Bake until a toothpick inserted into the center of the cake comes out clean, approximately 1 hour 15 minutes. Allow the cake to cool in the pan for 10 minutes. Brush the top of the cake with the orange juice. Transfer the cake to a wire rack and allow it to cool completely before dusting with powdered sugar.

Quick blanch whole, raw almonds by covering them with boiling water for 1 minute. Drain the water then squeeze each almond between your thumb and forefinger. The skin will slide right off. Allow the almonds to dry completely before toasting them.

To toast the almonds, place them in a single layer on an ungreased baking sheet. Bake in an oven preheated to 325°F/163°C until lightly browned, about 10-15 minutes, shaking the sheet frequently to promote even toasting. Cool completely before processing.

TOASTED RICE PUDDING

serves 4

Rice pudding is a dish with a long history of comforting tummies and nourishing souls the world over. Virtually every area on earth has its own variation, the most basic of ingredients (milk, rice and sugar) at its core. It's no coincidence that when a person describes their own preparation, they will often caress their belly and smile lovingly as if reveling in a flow of nostalgic memories. Rice pudding is undeniably a timeless and universal comfort food.

Prep Time: 5 minutes
Cook Time: 45 minutes
Vegan (options), Gluten Free

3 cups	milk of choice (cow, soy, nut, or rice)
⅓ cup	rice, uncooked
¼ cup	raisins
⅓ cup	sugar
1 teaspoon	vanilla essence or paste
⅛ teaspoon	nutmeg powder

Pour the rice into a dry skillet over medium heat. Toast the rice until nicely browned, about 4-5 minutes, shaking the pan frequently to promote even toasting. Remove the rice from the heat and set it aside.

Pour the milk into a medium sized saucepan and bring to a boil. Stir in the rice and raisins, reduce the heat to low and cover. Continue to cook until the rice is tender, about 30 minutes, stirring occasionally. Once the rice is tender, continue to cook uncovered until the pudding takes on a creamy texture, about 10 more minutes, stirring frequently. Stir in the sugar and vanilla and cook for 1 minute longer.

Portion the rice pudding into serving dishes and garnish with nutmeg.

Serve warm or chilled.

Any rice variety can be used though many people prefer to use a short grain such as Italian arborio rice (commonly used for risotto) because the high natural starch content lends itself to a very creamy pudding, Just note that brown and wild rice varieties will require some additional cooking time.

Black rice porridge with banana, an Indonesian variation.

COCONUT OAT BARS

makes 9 bars

This recipe is adapted from one of my long time bar cookie favorites, Butterscotch Brownies from Betty Crocker's Cooky Book These have the same firm edge and chewy center, but incorporate a hardy tropical twist.

Prep Time: 15 minutes
Cook Time: 20 minutes
Vegan

⅔ cup	coconut oil
1 cup (8 oz.)	brown sugar
⅓ cup	tofu
1 teaspoon	vanilla essence or paste
⅔ cup (3⅓ oz.)	atta or flour of choice
1 cup (3 oz.)	whole rolled oats
⅓ cup (1 oz.)	coconut, dried and shredded
¾ teaspoon	baking soda
½ teaspoon	salt

Preheat the oven to 350°F/176°C.

Lightly oil a 9x9x3-inch baking dish and set it aside.

In a large bowl, whisk together the oil, sugar, tofu and vanilla until well combined.

In a separate bowl, combine the flour, oats, coconut, baking soda and salt.

Stir the dry ingredients into the wet until all ingredients are even distributed. The mixture will be slightly stiff.

Transfer the mixture to the prepared baking dish and spread into an even layer. For this, I like to pat the mixture with damp hands.

Bake for 20 minutes or until just browned.

Cool in the baking dish for 10 minutes then cut into bars.

Store cookies in an airtight container.

TIL CHIKKI
(SESAME SEED BRITTLE)

makes about 24 pieces

This delicious brittle candy originates mainly from the western Indian state of Maharashtra, but is popular throughout the whole of India as well as its neighboring countries. Its available in an incredible variety of flavors spanning from the more traditional peanut or almond to the exotic like rose petal or mint. I am partial to the sesame seed variety because it reminds me of my boisterous and loveable friend, Norah. The two of us were roommates at an ashram in Trimbek, and would often nibble on sesame chikki as we giggled our way right up to the early evening lights out.

Prep Time: 5 minutes + 30 minutes cooling time
Cook Time: 10 minutes
Vegan, Gluten Free

1 teaspoon	ghee or butter, plus additional for greasing
⅔ cup (3½ oz.)	jaggery
1 cup (4 oz.)	sesame seeds, toasted

As with most candy, chikki preparation is very much a matter of timing. The changes in the syrup occur quickly, so prepare your space before you begin. You don't want to be distracted at a crucial moment in the process.

If you choose to toast the sesame seeds yourself (for instructions, refer to side note on p.108), allow them to cool completely before beginning the chikki preparation.

Lightly grease a sheet pan and set it aside along with a rolling pin.

Heat the ghee or butter in a medium sized pan over medium-low heat. Add the jaggery. Stir continuously as the jaggery melts into a syrup and begins to bubble. As the syrup approaches hard-ball stage, the color will lighten slightly and the bubbles will become more plentiful. If you are using a candy/fry thermometer, this stage occurs at 260°F/127°C. To test if the syrup has reached hard-ball stage, drop a small globule of it into cool water. If the globule forms a hard ball, very resistant to a firm squeeze, then it has arrived.

From hard-ball stage, continue to cook the jaggery syrup for 30-45 seconds. When it begins to darken in color, it is entering the soft crack stage, 270°F/132°C. Immediately remove the pan from the heat, stir in the sesame seeds and pour the mixture out onto the prepared sheet pan. Roll the mixture out to about ¼-inch thick. Immediately use a large knife or cleaver to cut the chikki into pieces. Allow the chikki to finish cooling completely before enjoying.

Store the chikki in a sealed container.

DATE BALLS

makes about 2½ dozen balls

Dates are one of the world's earliest treats, requiring no preparation yet fit for a king. Now, I do realize there tends to be a certain emotional thud that accompanies the mention of date balls these days. They can carry an undertone of ordinary, evident, maybe even homely, but these no-bake date balls are an enchanting way to rediscover the magnificent date.

Prep Time: 20 minutes
Cook Time: 0 minutes
Vegan, Gluten Free

1 cup (6½ oz.)	dried dates, pitted
1 cup (3½ oz.)	walnuts or nut of choice
¼ cup (¾ oz.)	cocoa powder
½ teaspoon	vanilla paste or essence
½ cup (1¼ oz.)	coconut, dried and ground or shredded, for rolling

Using a food processor, process the nuts to a semi coarse powder then transfer them to a medium sized bowl and set them aside.

Again using a food processor, process the dates into a very thick paste using a small amount of water if necessary. Add the date paste to the walnuts along with the cocoa powder and vanilla. Stir until the mixture comes together and the ingredients are evenly distributed. You may need to knead the mixture a couple of times using your hands. Scoop out a tablespoon size portion of mixture, roll into a ball then roll in coconut to coat. Repeat for the remainder of the mixture.

Serve cool or room temperature.

Store in a sealed container, refrigeration is optional.

LOADED CARROT BREAD

makes 1 loaf

Quick breads are the equal opportunity employer of the sweet world. Easy and adaptable in nature, they ensure that anybody can shine like a baking rock star. This carrot bread bakes some of autumn's rich colors and signature spices into a tender loaf eager to please.

Prep Time: 20 minutes
Cook Time: 50 minutes

¾ cup (5½ oz.)	sugar
½ cup	oil
2	eggs
1 teaspoon	vanilla essence or paste
1 cup (5 oz.)	atta or flour of choice
2 teaspoons	cinnamon powder
1 teaspoon	baking soda
¾ teaspoon	salt
½ pound	carrots, peeled and shredded (about 3 cups prepared)
2 teaspoons	ginger, minced or micro-planed
½ cup (4¼ oz.)	raisins
½ cup (2 oz.)	walnuts, chopped

Preheat the oven to 350°F/176°C.

Grease and flour an 8½x4½x3½-inch loaf pan.

In a medium bowl, whisk together the sugar, oil, eggs and vanilla until pale yellow.

In a separate bowl, combine the flour, cinnamon, baking soda and salt. Add the carrots, ginger, raisins and walnuts and toss until all the carrots are nicely coated. Using a rubber spatula, fold the carrot mixture into the wet mixture until all the ingredients are just moist. Transfer the batter to the loaf pan.

Bake for 50 minutes or until a toothpick inserted into the center comes out clean. Allow the loaf to cool in the pan for 30 minutes before turning it out onto a wire rack to cool completely.

When the bread is done it should spring back when you touch the surface of its center lightly with your finger. If it springs back, use a toothpick to be sure it's done. Insert a toothpick in the center of the bread and hold it there for a second before pulling it out. If a couple of crumbs stick to the toothpick, the bread is done; if you see a wet batter, give your bread another 5 minutes before checking it again.

ANISE-ORANGE BISCOTTI

makes about 1½ dozen

Homemade biscotti, like most things homemade, are nothing like their commercial counterparts. The way my mom puts it, biscotti should never put you at risk of breaking a tooth. Although sturdy enough to dunk in coffee or port wine, these biscotti have an elegant crumble like no other. With subtle sweetness and old world flavor these twice-baked biscuits make a thoughtful gift or offering for company and the aroma will linger long after the oven has been turned off.

Prep Time: 20 minutes
Cook Time: 50 minutes

2 cups (10 oz.)	all purpose flour
1½ teaspoon	baking powder
1 cup (7 oz.)	sugar
⅛ teaspoon	salt
1 tablespoon	anise seed, crushed
2	eggs
1	egg yolk
1 tablespoon	anise flavor liqueur or anise extract
1 tablespoon	orange zest

Preheat the oven to 350°F/176°C.

Some common varieties of anise flavor liqueurs include arak (Arabia), anisette and pastis (France), anesone and sambuca (Italy), herbsaint (U.S.A.) and ouzo (Greece).

To make your own anise extract, fill a small jar with whole star anise then top with vodka or bourbon. Allow the extract to mature for a minimum of 2 weeks before using.

Lightly grease and flour a baking sheet.

In a large bowl, combine the flour, baking powder, sugar, salt and anise seeds. Form a well in the center and add the eggs, egg yolk, liqueur or extract and zest. Using your hand or a wooden spoon, stir until the ingredients come together. Turn the dough out onto a clean, lightly floured surface. Knead the dough a few times just to make the dough smooth and consistent throughout.

Divide the dough into two equal portions. Roll each portion into a log approximately 7 inches long. Place the logs cross-wise on the baking sheet. Slightly flatten the tops of the logs until the width measures about 3 inches.

Bake the flattened logs for 35 minutes. Remove them from the oven and reduce the oven temperature to 300°F/149°C.

Allow the logs to cool on racks for about 20 minutes then use a sharp serrated knife to cut them into ¼-inch slices. It is a nice touch to cut these slices on a slight bias. Return the slices to the baking sheets cut side down.

Bake for 16 more minutes flipping the biscotti over after the first 8 minutes.
The final biscotti should be golden in color and crispy-dry.

Cool biscotti completely on wire a rack before storing them in a sealed
container.

CHOCOLATE CAKE WITH FUDGE ICING

makes 1 cake or about 20 cupcakes

Ask my husband to bake you a cake, and this is most definitely the one you will get. It's his go-to cake recipe, coincidentally found on the back of most Hershey's Cocoa boxes. Though I've developed a few variations, there's simply no need to reinvent the wheel here. Dependably moist and classically chocolate, this cake is a sure thing.

Prep Time: 15 minutes
Cook Time: 35 minutes (may vary depending on your pan option)

FOR THE CAKE

2 cups (14 oz.)	sugar
1 ¾ cup (8¾ oz.)	all-purpose flour
¾ cup (2¼ oz.)	unsweetened cocoa powder
1½ teaspoon	baking powder
1½ teaspoon	baking soda
1 teaspoon	salt
2	eggs
1 cup	milk of choice (cow, soy, nut, rice, buttermilk or yogurt)
½ cup	oil
1 cup	boiling water

FOR THE ICING

½ cup (4 oz.)	butter, melted
⅔ cup (2 oz.)	unsweetened cocoa powder
¼ teaspoon	salt
3 cups (13 oz.)	powdered sugar
⅓ cup	milk of choice (cow, soy, nut, rice, buttermilk)

Preheat the oven to 350°F/176°C (this is the same for all variations).

Grease and flour two 9-inch round baking pans.

In a medium bowl, combine the sugar, flour, cocoa, baking powder, baking soda and salt. In a separate, larger bowl, whisk together the eggs, milk, and oil. Add the dry ingredients to the wet and stir until combined. Stir in the boiling water. The batter will be very thin. Divide the batter equally into the prepared pans.

Bake for 30-35 minutes or until a toothpick inserted in center comes out clean. Cool the cakes for 20 minutes before turning them out onto a wire rack to cool completely.

For the fudge icing, add the cocoa and salt to the butter and stir with a whisk until smooth. In a separate bowl, whisk together the powdered sugar and milk until thick and smooth. Add the butter-cocoa mixture to the sugar-milk mixture and stir thoroughly with a whisk until a spreadable consistency is attained. Spread on the cooled cake.

FLAVOR VARIATIONS

Intense Cinnamon Chocolate Cake: Add 3 tablespoons cinnamon powder to the dry ingredients of the cake plus 2 tablespoons along with the cocoa in the frosting.

Café Coffee Chocolate Cake: Substitute 1 cup of freshly brewed hot coffee for the boiling water in the cake batter. Add 1 tablespoon of coffee to the butter-cocoa mixture in the frosting and decrease the milk to 5 tablespoons. Note: The coffee used in the frosting does not need to be hot and can be reserved from that which is brewed for use in the cake.

SHAPE VARIATIONS

One-Pan Cake: Grease and flour a 13x9x2-inch baking dish. Pour the batter into the prepared pan. Bake for 35 to 40 minutes. Allow the cake to cool completely before frosting.

Three-Layer Cake: Grease and flour three 8-inch round baking pans. Divide the batter evenly into the prepared pans. Bake for 30 to 35 minutes. Cool the cakes for 10 minutes before turning them out onto a wire rack. Allow the cakes to cool completely before frosting.

Bundt Cake: Grease and flour 12-cup Bundt pan. Pour the batter into the prepared pan. Bake for 50 to 55 minutes. Cool the cake for 15 minutes before turning it out onto a wire rack. Allow the cake to cool completely before frosting.

Cupcakes (makes about 20-2 ounce cupcakes): Lightly grease a standard muffin tin or line it with paper baking cups. Fill each slot 2/3 full with the batter. Bake for 22-24 minutes. Allow the cakes to cool completely before frosting.

WHIRLEY POP KETTLE CORN

makes about 6 quarts

If you're like me and love stovetop prepared popcorn, but could due without all the stove side shaking and shimmying, a Whirley Pop popcorn popper is your answer. A turn crank on the handle spins the stirring system via two simple gear mechanisms and the corn is kept moving across the bottom of the pan, for even heat and oil distribution. A mere 3 minutes of cranking gives you a big bowl of fluffy, crisp sweet corn. Queue up the movie. I'll meet you on the couch.

Prep Time: 2 minutes
Cook Time: 3 minutes
Vegan, Gluten Free

¼ cup	oil
½ cup	pop corn kernels
¼ cup	raw sugar
	salt

Whirley Pop poppers can be purchased at numerous shops and websites. The manufacturer also accepts orders directly via their website, popcornpopper.com

Place a large bowl and all your pre-measured ingredients within your reach by the stove. Place the whirley popper over medium-high heat. Pour the oil, corn kernels and sugar into the popper. Begin stirring steadily. Once the kernels begin to pop, stir briskly until the popping stops. Carefully empty the kettle corn into your bowl and sprinkle lightly with salt.

VARIATIONS

Plain Jane:

¼ cup	oil
½ cup	pop corn kernels
¼ cup	raw sugar
	salt

Carmel Corn:

¼ cup	oil
½ cup	pop corn kernels
2 tablespoons	raw sugar
2 tablespoons	dark brown sugar
	salt

Cracker Jack King:

¼ cup	oil
½ cup	pop corn kernels
2 tablespoons	raw sugar
2 tablespoons	dark brown sugar
⅓ cup	raw almonds*
	salt

For easy clean up, fill the popper with hot water and a couple of drops of detergent. Allow it to soak while you enjoy your corn and there will be no scrubbing required when you return.

*Quickly open the lid of the popper and add the almonds only after the corn kernels have begun popping. This will prevent the almonds from burning.

MUESLI

makes about 3 quarts

Perhaps a bit of a stretch to include this one in the 'Sweets' section and yet, here it is. A bowl of muesli is a superb illustration of just how much the earth offers us and making your own can make you feel instantly healthy, clever and capable. I'm quite sure that I've never made the same mixture twice which is why this is more of a formula than a recipe.

Prep Time: 15 minutes
Cook Time: 0 minutes
Vegan

8 cups	cereal
2½ cups	dried fruit
1½ cup	nuts
½ cup	seeds

Cereal:	*Dried Fruit:*	*Nuts:*
rolled oats	raisins	hazel nuts
rye flakes	sultans	flaked coconut
cereal flakes	currents	almond
wheat bran	berries	walnuts
barley kernels	banana chips	brazil nuts, chopped
	prunes, chopped	
	apples, chopped	*Seeds:*
	apricots, chopped	pumpkin seeds
	dates, chopped	sesame seeds
		sunflower seeds
		flax seeds

Combine your choice of ingredients and store in an airtight container.

Garnishes for Serving:
milk
yogurt
honey
fresh fruit
cinnamon

In cool weather, find simple comfort in a bowl of warm muesli. Pour boiling water or hot milk over muesli, cover and allow it to sit for 5 minutes before eating.

Opposite page: A local boy mans the sales counter at a tea plantation in the hills of Munnar, India

BEVERAGES

The cup that cheers !

It takes a rare combination of strength and delicate flavour to create the finest blend.

Unique Taste of
MUNNAR

PREMIUM DUST TEA

Ripple

KANAN DEVAN HILLS
PLANTATIONS COMPANY
PRIVATE LIMITED

The **Real** garden fresh TEA

MASALA CHAI
(SPICED TEA)

serves 2

As one of the world's largest tea producers, India maintains a rich tea drinking culture and a cup of hot, milky chai is rarely more than a street corner and a few rupees away. With as many masala mixtures and preparation methods for masala chai as there are chai wallas, I can say without a doubt, that there is no one right way to make this beautifully aromatic drink. But most Indians will agree that the tea powder should be boiled over sustained heat rather than steeped in water just cool of boiling. Regarded for giving the tea a 'stronger flavor,' this popular technique also happens to render its caffeine content comparable to that of coffee.

Prep Time: 2 minutes
Cook Time: 5 minutes
Vegan (options), Gluten Free

5	green cardamom pods
5	whole cloves
5	whole peppercorns
1	small stick of cinnamon
1½ cups	milk of choice (cow, soy, nut, rice)
½ cup	water
2 teaspoons	tea powder or 2 teabags
¼ teaspoon	ginger powder
1 tablespoon	sugar
⅛ teaspoon	nutmeg, micro-planed to garnish

Tea powder, also called tea dust, is tea that has been ground ultra fine. High quality tea powders are ground under low temperatures in order to retain their flavor.

I use whole cow's milk. If you any other milk option increase the amount of milk to 2 cups and omit the water.

Crack open the cardamom pods and remove the black seeds. Crush the seeds along with the cloves, peppercorns and cinnamon stick into a relatively fine powder. You can do this using a mortar and pestle or a few prolonged pulses in the coffee grinder.

Pour the milk, water and crushed spices into a saucepan over high heat. Just as the mixture begins to boil, add the tea, ginger and sugar.

As the tea boils, the mixture will froth up toward the top of the pan. When this happens, remove the pan from the heat, swirl or stir the mixture until it recedes then return the pan to the heat. Repeat this 2 more times before pouring the tea into cups through a fine mesh sieve.

Garnish with nutmeg and serve hot, hot, hot.

BANANA-DATE SMOOTHIE

serves 2-3

This drink is my slightly adulterated version of the simple date milk commonly used to break the daily fasts of Ramadan. It can hold its own against an ice cream milkshake and has stepped up to the dessert plate for me on many an occasion.

Prep Time: 5 minutes
Cook Time: 0 minutes
Vegan (options), Gluten Free

1½ cup	milk of choice (cow, soy, nut, rice)
6	large dates, pitted
3	medium bananas, peeled and frozen
1 teaspoon	vanilla essence or paste
⅛ teaspoon	salt (optional)
1 pinch	cinnamon powder, to garnish

Place all ingredients in blender. Blend until smooth.

Pour into glasses, garnish with cinnamon and serve immediately.

LIME SODA

serves 4

On summer days in India when the mercury soars and a distinct layer of dust torments your throat, there is nothing more refreshingly alluring than a glass of lime soda from a roadside vendor. Sold out of rickety carts amongst the bustle of rickshaws and speeding mopeds, bright displays of limes lure you towards forgetting one of the most fundamental rules for non-locals...do not drink the water. I just had to formulate my own anxiety-free version of lime soda. Here it is.

Prep Time: 10 minutes
Cook Time: 5 minutes
Vegan, Gluten Free

FOR THE SYRUP

2 tablespoons	water
¼ cup	sugar

FOR THE SODA

4 cups	soda water
½ cup	lime juice
½ teaspoon	black salt (can substitute regular salt)
12	mint leaves, whole or chopped

To make the syrup, combine the water and sugar in a saucepan over low heat. Stir continuously until the sugar is completely dissolved, about 3-5 minutes. Remove the syrup from the heat and set it aside to cool.

In a pitcher, combine the soda water, lime juice, salt and mint and stir well.

Serve the syrup along side the pitcher and iced glasses. People can add as much or as little syrup as they like.

AAM LASSI
(MANGO YOGURT DRINK)

serves 4

The mango can be substituted for equal parts of papaya, pineapple, banana, or whatever ripe fruit is calling to you.

Prep Time: 10 minutes
Cook Time: 0 minutes
Vegan (options), Gluten Free

2	mangoes, peeled, pitted and chopped
2 cups	yogurt
½ cup	milk of choice (cow, soy, nut, rice)
2 teaspoons	sugar (optional)
¼ teaspoon	vanilla essence or paste (optional)

Blend all ingredients together until smooth.

Serve cool.

CLARA
(LEMON BEER)

serves 2

Leave it to the Spaniards to come up with this clever way to cool off and chill out. Some call this popular summertime drink a Shandy, I just call it genius.

Prep Time: 2 minutes
Cook Time: 0 minutes
Vegan

1	12-ounce beer
1	12-ounce lemon soda, such as Fanta
2	12-ounce beer glasses, chilled

Light tasting beers such as uncomplicated lagers work best.

Divide the beer evenly amongst the two glasses. Slowly top them off with the lemon soda.

Bottoms up.

Opposite page: The enchanting face and all-knowing gaze of a beagle named Suki

DOG

PUMKPIN NUT DOG TREATS

makes about 9 dozen small treats

This one's for the dogs because few things can warm your heart the way an ear-to-ear furry faced smile can. This is a very tolerant dough that is moist and slightly springy, but still easy to roll out. With minimal effort, these treats immediately fill the house with the aroma of cinnamon as well as the tappa-tappa of happy hound feet.

Prep Time: 20 minutes
Cook Time: 45 minutes
Vegan

2 tablespoons	pumpkin purée
2 tablespoons	creamy nut butter
2 tablespoons	oil
½ cup	water
1½ cup (7½ oz.)	atta or flour of choice
1 teaspoons	cinnamon
pinch	salt

Preheat the oven to 350°F/176°C.

In a medium bowl, whisk together the pumpkin, nut butter, oil and water. Add the flour, cinnamon and salt and stir until the dough comes together nicely. Turn the dough out onto a clean, lightly floured surface and knead it a couple of times to get a workable texture, adding flour as needed.

Divide the dough in half. Roll out one of the halves into an ⅛-inch thick slab. Use a pizza or ravioli cutter to crosscut the slab into squares, about 1½x1½-inch.

Transfer the cut squares into an ungreased baking sheet. You need not leave much space in between each as these treats will puff slightly during baking rather than spread. Repeat the roll out process for the second half of dough.

Bake for 15-20 minutes or until very crispy and nicely browned.

The treats can be left on the baking sheet to cool completely before storing them in an airtight container.

"Yesterday I was a dog. Today I'm a dog. Tomorrow I'll probably still be a dog. Sigh! There's so little hope for advancement."

Snoopy

COOKING TIMES FOR DRIED BEANS, LENTILS, DAL & GRAINS

NOTE ABOUT SOAKING

In regards to the Cooking Time Chart on the following pages, though pressure cooking times are included for unsoaked beans, I highly recommended that all beans, unless otherwise indicated, be soaked prior to cooking. Soaking facilitates even cooking, decreases cooking time, and helps to break down oligosaccharides (the indigestible sugars that commonly cause gas) and other compounds that inhibit optimal nutrient and mineral absorption. The most effective soaking method is the natural method, also known as the long soak method, because it best preserves the integrity of the bean's structure during cooking.

Natural/Long Soak Method:
- Soak the beans in tepid water according to the Natural/Long Soaking Time indicated in the Cooking Time Chart.
- Drain and rinse the beans.
- Proceed with the recipe for soaked beans.

Pressure Cooker Quick Soak Method:
- Place the beans in the pressure cooker and cover with 3 inches of water. Bring the pressure cooker to full pressure. Decrease the heat to low and continue to cook for 5 minutes.
- Remove the pressure cooker from the heat and allow the pressure to drop naturally.
- Drain and rinse the beans.
- Proceed with the recipe for soaked beans.

Open Pot Quick Soak Method:
- Boil the beans in water for 3 minutes in a heavy pot.
- Cover and allow beans to soak for 2 hours.
- Drain and rinse the beans.
- Proceed with the recipe for soaked beans.

NOTE ABOUT COOKING TIMES

Cooking times may vary slightly, especially for beans and lentils as size, dryness and desired softness each play a factor. Cooking times for the conventional boiling method begin at boil. Cooking times for the pressure cooker method begin once full pressure is reached, that is to say once the cooker releases its first whistle. All pressure cooking times are based upon the natural release method in which the pressure is allowed to dissipate fully on its own prior to opening.

WHEN USING A PRESSURE COOKER, ALWAYS READ AND FOLLOW THE SAFETY GUIDELINES PROVIDED BY THE MANUFACTURER.

BEAN	NATURAL/LONG SOAKING TIME (MINIMUM)	CONVENTIONAL BOILING METHOD TIME (SOAKED)	PRESSURE COOKING TIME (SOAKED)	PRESSURE COOKING TIME (UNSOAKED)	COOKED YEILD
Adzuki	6 hours	50-60 min.	5-9 min.	14-20	3 x
Black Bean	4 hours	75-90 min.	4-6 min.	22-24	2¼ x
Black-Eyed Peas	-	45-60 min.	3 min.	6-7	2 x
Borlotti	6 hours	45-60 min.	7-10 min.	22-25	3 x
Cannellini	6 hours	60-90 min.	6-8 min.	25-30	2½ x
Chickpea	8 hours	120-240 min.	13-15 min.	35-40	2 x
Corona	6 hours	60-90 min.	8-10 min.	25-30	2⅔ x
Cranberry see Borlotti	-	-	-	-	-
Fava	10 hours	120-180 min.	12 min.	25-30	2⅔ x
Garbanzo see Chickpea	-	-	-	-	-
Great White Beans see Corona	-	-	-	-	-
Haricots see Cannellini	-	-	-	-	-
Kabuli see Chickpea	-	-	-	-	-
Kidney, red	6 hours	60 min.	13-15 min.	22-24	2¼ x
Kidney, white see Cannellini	-	-	-	-	-
Lima, small	4 hours	50-60 min.	5-7 min.	12-15	3 x
Lime, large	4 hours	60-90 min.	5-7 min.	12-15	2 x
Mung	4 hours	45-60 min.	5-7 min.	12-15	2 x
Navy	4 hours	45-60 min.	6-8 min.	18-20	2⅔ x
Peas, whole	-	40-45 min.	8-10 min.	16-18	2 x
Peas, split, green or yellow	-	30 min.	-	6-10 min.	2 x
Pigeon Peas see Peas, whole	-	-	-	-	-
Pinto	6 hours	60-90 min.	4-6 min.	22-24	2⅔ x
Romano see Borolitti	-	-	-	-	-
Scarlet Runner	10 hours	75-90 min.	5-8 min.	18-20	2 x
Soy, black	12 hours	180-200 min.	22-25 min.	35-40	3 x
Soy, yellow	12 hours	120-180 min.	20-22 min.	35-40	3 x
Soy, red see Adzuki	-	-	-	-	2 x
White see Navy	-	-	-	-	2 x

The Paisley Palate Cookbook

LENTILS	CONVENTIONAL BOILING METHOD TIME	PRESSURE COOKING TIME	COOKED YEILD
Masoor	18-22 min.	4-6 min.	2¼ x
Puy, French green	25-30 min.	7-9 min.	2¼ x
Regular, brown/ green	35-40 min.	8-10 min.	2¼ x
Urad	25-30 min.	10-12 min.	2¼ x

DAL	CONVENTIONAL BOILING METHOD TIME	PRESSURE COOKING TIME	COOKED YEILD
Channa	30 min.	7-8	2½ x
Masoor	20 min.	5-6	2½ x
Mung Dal	20 min.	5-6	2½ x
Toor Dal	25 min.	6-7	2½ x
Urad	20 min.	5-6	2½ x

RICE	RICE:WATER RATIO	TRADITIONAL BOILING METHOD TIME	PRESSURE COOKING TIME	COOKED YEILD
Brown Rice, Long Grain: *Basmati* *Jasmine*	1:2.25	45-50 min.	16 min.	3 x
Brown Rice: Medium Grain	1:2.25	35-40 min.	15 min.	3 x
Brown Rice, Short Grain	1:2.25	45-50 min.	16 min.	3 x
White Rice: Short Grain	1:1.5	20-30 min.	8 min.	3 x
White Rice: Medium Grain	1:1.5	20-30 min.	7min.	3 x
White Rice: Long Grain *Basmati* *Jasmine* *Texmati*	1:1.5	20-25 min.	4 min.	3 x
Wild Rice: *Manomen*	1:3	50-60 min.	20-22 min.	3 x

OTHER WHOLE GRAINS	GRAIN:WATER RATIO	CONVENTIONAL BOILING METHOD TIME	PRESSURE COOKING TIME	COOKED YEILD
Amaranth	1:2.5	20-25 min.	9 min.	2½ x
Barley, Flakes	1:2	15-17 min.	9 min.	2½ x
Barley, Pearl	1:4.5	25-30 min.	15-16 min.	3½ x
Barley, Whole	1:3	60-70 min.	30-35 min.	3½ x
Buckwheat, Untoasted	1:2	20-30 min.	12 min.	3 x
Buckwheat, Kasha	1:2	15-20 min.	7-9 min.	3 x
Kamut	1:3	60-80 min.	20-30 min.	2½ x
Millet	1:2	20-30 min.	9 min.	3½ x
Oats, Rolled	1:4	10 min.	5 min.	1¾ x
Oats, Steel Cut	1:4	20-40 min.	10 min.	3 x
Oats, Whole (Oat Groats)	1:3	45-60 min.	15-18 min.	3½ x
Quinoa	1:2	15-20 min.	6 min.	2¾ x
Rye Berries	1:4	60 min.	15-20 min.	3 x
Spelt, Berries	1:3.5	90 min.	20-25 min.	2½ x
Teff	1:3	20 min.	5 min.	3½ x
Wheat, Berries	1:3	90-120 min.	32-35 min.	2½ x
Wheat, Cracked	1:3	20-25 min.	10-12 min.	2¼ x
Wheat, Bulgar	1:2	10-15min.	8-10 min.	2½ x

The Paisley Palate Cookbook

INDEX

Jennifer Syler is a registered dietitian and certified hatha yoga teacher who currently resides outside of New Delhi, India with her husband Brad, son Walter and beagle Suki.

Made in the USA
Lexington, KY
09 September 2014